Beyond Startup Week

What First-Time Entrepreneurs
Don't Know to Ask

Beyond Startup Week

WHAT FIRST-TIME ENTREPRENEURS DON'T KNOW TO ASK

MICHELLE MINK, M.S.

SEE Publishing

ISBN # 978-1-932491-03-6 Paperback
ISBN # 978-1-932491-04-3 E-book
ISBN # 978-1-932491-05-0 E-book (Enhanced Version with Color)

This print edition was first published in June 2023

Thanks to my great team of contributors and editors:

Michelle Barnes, editor (mbarnes_ny@yahoo.com)
Denise Gibbon, legal review (Above the Dotted Line)
Barbara McNichol, editor (Barbara McNichol Editorial)
Book Baby, editorial staff (BookBaby.com)
Cathi Stevenson, cover designer (bookcoverexpress.com)

SEE Publishing
www.SEEpubs.com

CONTENTS

So, You Want to be an Entrepreneur

When you ask people to describe a typical entrepreneur, many think of a twenty-something guy in a hoodie banging out code — perhaps creating an app, a social media site or a software program. Who can blame them? Real-life fairy-tale stories like that make for great articles, books, TV shows and movies.

In reality, the average Emma and Ernie Entrepreneur start dry-cleaning services, auto repair shops, hair and nail salons, restaurants, Etsy stores, souvenir shops and other popular consumer businesses, not to mention those providing services to other enterprises. It's also more typical for people to start businesses when they're in the 35 to 64 age range rather than being college dropouts not legally old enough to drink alcohol. Research from Ewing Marion Kauffman Foundation shows that since 2006, most new U.S. businesses are started by people 35 years old and older.[1]

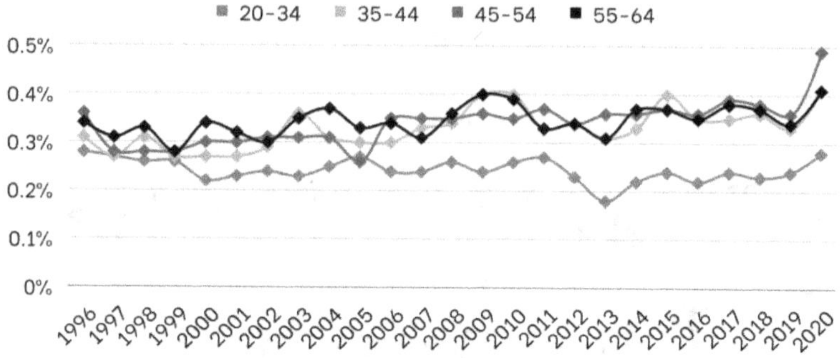

A decade or more of work experience instills confidence, allows time to establish a professional network and provides a strong real-world knowledge foundation for business success. While this helps with day-to-day operations, many missed details unique to birthing a business can result in delays, wasted resources and burning through valuable cash. For startup entrepreneurs, not getting their ducks in a row early can snowball into big problems down the road.

Many people turn startups into successful businesses, but many others end up shuttering their doors for a multitude of reasons. "The Top 12 Reasons Startups Fail", published by CB Insights, continually tracks the self-identified causes of business failures in hopes of educating new entrepreneurs so they can avoid similar fates.

Why Businesses Fail

Management Issues

- Not the Right Team = 14%
- Disharmony Among Team/Investors = 7%
- Burned Out/Lack of Passion = 5%

Financial Challenges

- Ran Out of Cash/Failed to Raise New Capital = 38%
- Pricing/Cost Issues = 15%

Product & Market Challenges

- Got Outcompeted = 20%
- Product Mistimed = 10%
- Poor Product = 8%

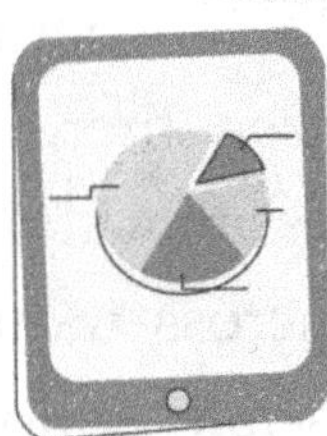

Planning Missteps

- No Market Need = 35%
- Flawed Business Model = 19%
- Regulatory/Legal Challenges = 18%
- Pivot Gone Bad = 6%

"The Top 12 Reasons Startups Fail", published by CB Insights

(Note: The total doesn't add up to one hundred percent because multiple answers were allowed.[2])

Many of these challenges could've been minimized or avoided altogether if the new entrepreneurs had taken some basic steps starting out. A multitude of helpful resources is available, but trying to figure out what's important and applicable can feel like drinking from a fire hose.

Successful entrepreneurs understand the difficulty of launching and growing a company, so many want to share their knowledge. That's why the number of startup programs and events has exploded over the last decade, providing tools, training, education and networking for those facing the challenges of piloting a young business.

Such events are attended by those who are formulating an idea, just opening their doors, in growth mode, looking for funding or in any other stage of starting a business. Typically, multiple instructional tracks are offered, focusing on a particular industry, life cycle stage or functional area (e.g., marketing, customer service, payments/billing). These are great for finding out about resources, understanding business challenges and making local connections.

The inspiration for creating this book was born after attending various startup events and experiencing entrepreneurship several times over. I realized there was a common set of activities for every new business that should be checked off, but the approach is different across industries. Instead of capturing the details of every possible option in a thousand-page paperweight, I narrowed it to a handful of the most popular business types. In this book, we'll follow five fictional newbie founders from their happenstance meeting at a local startup event to officially launching their imaginary companies into the world.

As you'll see, I provide relevant data and resources followed by questions to help guide these enthusiastic entrepreneurs through an exciting startup journey complete with homework assignments and group discussions. Your startup adventure might align perfectly with one of our entrepreneurs, or it might be more beneficial to cherry-pick the pieces that work best for your situation.

Are you ready for an exciting trip through the land of entrepreneurship? Let's start our fictitious story by heading over to the local Startup Week where I was one of the organizers, coordinated one of the event tracks, and presented at or facilitated multiple sessions.

The Gathering

I'm meandering about the noisy open space at the Startup Week's closing party after completing all presentations and coordinator obligations. Enjoying the electricity in the room, I spot an animated group gathered around one of the tall stand-up tables. Attracted to their enthusiasm and emboldened by the room's positive energy, I walk over to hear what's stoking their excitement. I find out they're all newbie entrepreneurs trying to navigate the challenges of starting a business. Each attended Startup Week not knowing what to expect but hoping to pick up valuable nuggets of information. However, I quickly learn all five are overwhelmed by the amount of information delivered and unsure how to apply it.

I understand how they feel. With so many different things to consider when running a business, aspiring entrepreneurs can feel like cooped-up dogs let off leash to chase one squirrel after another. How should they prioritize? Which ideas and recommendations work best for their businesses? What resources can help along the way? What's the best way to evaluate new ideas?

Having been a part of multiple startup businesses and a leader of Startup Week, I introduce myself and briefly share my résumé highlights. Then I tell them about my program that guides first time entrepreneurs through the process of setting up a business using a simple step-by-step process in a safe peer supported environment. I suggest they join together and all emphatically agree. With everyone in, we schedule our first meeting for the following Monday evening. As leader, I set the tone by asking them to do some prep work.

"Prepare for our first meeting," I say, "by digesting and organizing the information you've gathered over the past week. Based on what you've learned, create a short one or two-sentence description of your business idea. That should include your product or service, who will use it, where it will be sold and how your customers will consume it. For example, *I want to start a fondue and chocolate shop that also rents and sells party supplies online with a retail storefront located in Orange County, California.*

ASSIGNMENT 1
Conceptualize Your Business Idea

1) Explain in a sentence or two what your business idea will be by identifying:

    a. What you will sell.
    b. Who will buy it.
    c. How they will get it.
    d. What it will do for your customers.

Chapter 2

Buckle Up for a Wild Ride

I begin Monday's meeting this way: "Welcome to a new adventure and wild ride crazier than Disney's Mr. Toad's! I'm very excited to see what your impact on the world will be. Let's start with introductions. Please share your name, what inspired you to jump into the startup world, and the kind of business you want to open. Who wants to go first?"

"Hi, I'm **Jade** and I have a passion for cooking. Creating new food flavors and trying twists on traditional recipes is what I do for fun. Friends and family bribe me with wine and artisanal coffee for an invitation to my imaginative dinners. I'm leaning toward starting a type of Asian fusion barbecue food place since those dishes seem to have the most popular and unique flavors. I've never been in the restaurant business, but I did win a second-place ribbon at a local barbecue competition. At this point, I'm not sure if a stand-alone restaurant, food truck, food court, catering business or something else is the way I want to go."

"Thanks, Jade. Now, my stomach's growling! This process we're starting will help you narrow down which of those options is the best for your situation," I explain. "Who wants to go next?"

"I will. My name is **Malik,** and it's only a matter of time before I'll be laid off from a startup company. I'm part of the engineering team in charge of designing a project management app. But it looks like the business won't make it despite the founders' efforts, so it's time for me to move on. This wasn't my first startup rodeo. I feel like I'm ready to venture out on my own but not sure what direction to go. I have all these different ideas swirling around in my head. It might be best to start by freelancing to pay the bills until I get a sharper focus on what business to start. It'll also give me time to flesh out ideas and decide what will inspire me to take that leap. At this point, I'm a little gun-shy."

"Completely understandable, Malik," I respond. "To overcome the hesitancy, it helps to think of those experiences as educational opportunities. Take a step back and analyze key inflection points in the life of those startups, looking at both internal challenges and external factors. Think of it as your own personal startup road map.

"In fact, it would be beneficial to create a list that includes four categories for each inflection noting the challenge, outcome, influencing factors and how the situation could've been handled differently. Choose things that, in hindsight, were turning points for you and/or the startup business. Events tend to get fuzzy over time, so this will be a good way to capture the details and apply the lessons learned down the road. Our experiences are only failures if we don't learn and grow from them. Who's next?"

"Hey, I'm **Dylan** and I've been an animal lover all my life. I've jumped around from job to job with no idea what to do. So, a couple of weeks ago, I was hangin' with friends, drinking wine on Friday night. We started talking about how dope it would be to work with animals instead of humans all day. Right?" Dylan cocked her head and gestured with open hands. "We all wanted to work at the zoo, but it's super hard to get a job there. I've done random stuff like dog walker and pet sitter, but that's just gig money. As we quaffed more vino, we did come up with some lit ideas: dog nannies/trainers for the über-wealthy, workout gyms for pups and people, travel adventures for dogs and their humans, a pet resort and spa, and a dating app for people with pets. I'm not sure how to figure out which idea might be best and what to do next."

"All those ideas sound super fun," I reply. "We'll work our way through the process of figuring out which option is the best fit so everyone can get to 'lighting up that OPEN sign.' Traditional banks aren't the only way to finance new ventures, so we'll explore unconventional ways to fund businesses, too. Next?"

"I'm **Andres** and I get amped designing gadgets and electronics. It's like how I feel when catching a rad wave. To pay the bills, I write code as a contractor, which is okay because I get to work on a bunch of different pumping projects. I'm not looking to quit contract gigs just yet, but I have a bunch of rando inventions I think could make money. The problem is figuring out which ones to move on and how to do it."

"There are different ways to bring products to market," I comment. "But the important things are to protect your ideas and to identify *all* the costs compared to what people will pay to figure out if any of your inventions can make money.

"And last but certainly not least," I nod toward the last group member.

"Hey everyone. I'm **Kaya** and I've been in health care since college but have gotten to the point of total frustration and burn-out. Plus, I want to have more control over my schedule and feel energized about work again. Some of my friends and coworkers have talked about creating an online wellness marketplace, but I'm fascinated by the possibilities of using artificial intelligence or other technologies to improve in-home health care. A friend of a friend is a techie, and we've been kicking around ideas. Mostly, I want to get a better understanding of what our next steps would be to create a real business."

"That sounds very intriguing, Kaya," I comment. "Creating unique solutions using proprietary technology tools can provide a marketing edge against competitors *and* a significant barrier to entry, which is important to investors. We'll eventually get into partnerships, organizational structure, funding and intellectual property (also known as IP), which are all important issues for the types of businesses you and others are considering.

"What a diverse and exciting group we have on our shared startup journey! I'm psyched! Now let me ask you this: Who enjoyed writing research papers in high school or college? Anyone? No one? Well, me neither. I think the MBA-toting 'experts' who were forced to complete business plans while in college want to inflict the same pain on others in the real world. Putting together a traditional business plan when starting out is a surefire way to zap your energy and spend a ton of time on a document that will be out of date in six to eighteen months.

"Instead, we're focusing on the *components* of your business and becoming an expert on your new baby. Just like every person on the planet is unique, so is your business. *Nobody else is selling the same product or service at the same price and time in the same places to the same people with the same resources.* The key to success is finding your profitable niche, so, constantly monitoring and analyzing the world around us is a good habit to get into. Planning and strategizing aren't exercises you do once or at the end of each year and then put on a shelf. They must become a habit, like physically training for a race or an outdoor adventure. Control the things you can, prepare for the things you can't and don't confuse the two," I conclude.

"Okay. Enough philosophizing. Let's roll up our sleeves and get to it. Your first assignment is to more clearly define what the business looks like."

Assignment Prep:
Define Your Business

"The first step is to figure out who your customers are, what need your business fulfills and what other options are out there," I explain. "Once you figure out your niche, go into it with a flexible mindset. That way, you're ready to quickly move the business in a different direction if things aren't working out as expected or unforeseen changes arise. All kinds of random acts can affect your business unexpectedly. Most people didn't foresee the dot-com bubble bursting, 9/11 happening or the 2008 housing market imploding. We can't control random acts of Mother Nature, presidential elections, trade embargoes or pandemics. What can we control? Creating distinctive customer relationships and establishing a solid business foundation that is flexible enough to quickly adapt to changes."

To help them visualize what I'm saying, I put up a poster on my portable easel. "You start with a product or service idea, then build business components and processes around it to create a unique user experience. By doing that, you'll crystallize how you're offering is different than everything else out there. Here's what those components look like." Then I point to a poster listing the main components of a business.

BUSINESS COMPONENTS

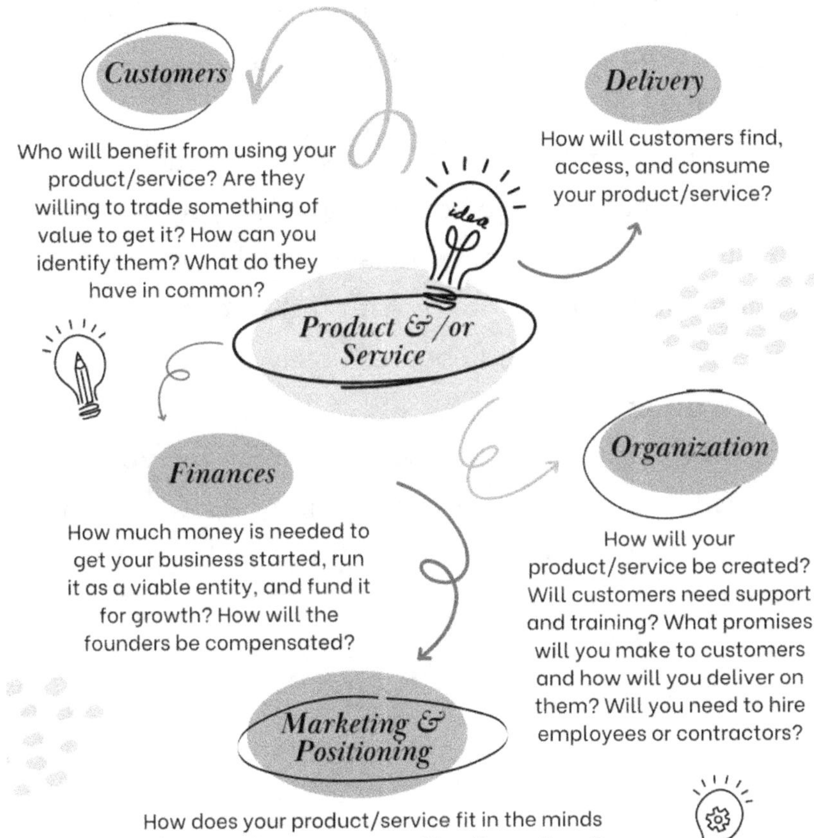

Customers — Who will benefit from using your product/service? Are they willing to trade something of value to get it? How can you identify them? What do they have in common?

Delivery — How will customers find, access, and consume your product/service?

Finances — How much money is needed to get your business started, run it as a viable entity, and fund it for growth? How will the founders be compensated?

Organization — How will your product/service be created? Will customers need support and training? What promises will you make to customers and how will you deliver on them? Will you need to hire employees or contractors?

Marketing & Positioning — How does your product/service fit in the minds of your customers compared to other options? Does it provide a positive feeling, reduction of fear, some level of status, or something else?

"Don't worry about understanding all of these pieces right now. We'll step through exercises that address each one in easily digestible chunks. This poster provides a high-level look at the moving parts so you have an idea of what we'll be covering.

"For our first roll-up-your-sleeves meeting, your homework assignment is to home in on what your business will be. You all have a good general idea of that, but the details need to be tightened up. To help with this, let's complete the following steps on the whiteboard," I say as I move toward it and start writing.

"If you're still grappling with specifics for your startup business, identify what you can for now. As we go through the process, your most viable opportunity will naturally come into focus."

ASSIGNMENT 2
Further Define the Business Idea

1) Explain what you want to sell or offer in one or two sentences.

2) Estimate how long it will take to start delivering your product or service to customers — one month, six months, two years, etc. If unsure, identify your target time frame.

3) In general, describe how you want to deliver your product or service. Will it be through a physical brick-and-mortar space (e.g., retail store, restaurant, office, coworking space), online, at the customer's location (e.g., landscaping, interior design), using a third party (e.g., distributor, aggregator like Amazon) or a combination of methods?

Chapter 3

Defining the Widget

"Welcome to the first step in bringing your idea to life," I begin at our second meeting. "As a refresher, the task at hand is to clarify what each business will look like. Let's go around the room and have each of you describe the idea, estimated time frame for turning on the OPEN sign, and how you'll get the offer into customers' hands.

"Remember, this is a starting point with no right or wrong answer. What you say won't be tattooed on your forehead. When running a business, the one constant is that the world keeps changing, so as you learn more about the market and opportunities, your business will shift in various ways."

Jade jumps in first. "I plan to cook and sell Asian fusion barbecue food based on what friends and family have told me they like, along with a few competition recipe ideas. I'll start there and learn as things go along. As to where, maybe I start with a food truck or pop-up part-time to get my feet wet and prove to myself I can do it. I've saved some money and talked to people about their experiences, so I'm probably looking at three to six months out before I make the big leap full-time. My ultimate goal is to open a brick-and-mortar restaurant but to start, I'll go with either the food truck or the pop-up route."

"I'll go next," **Malik** says. "I'm going to provide engineering management services on a project basis. A common need is technical expertise to help fill gaps on projects running three to eighteen months in length, so I'll go after those opportunities. I've been talking with a few colleagues about contract gigs and will probably do that while working to set up a full-blown business. The work would mostly be done using a computer and phone connected to the internet, so I can deliver on projects remotely from anywhere. Occasionally, I'll need to meet clients face-to-face, but that will either be at their location or a neutral site."

"Okay," pipes in **Dylan**, "so I'm totally into starting a dog grooming, training, or kenneling business of some kind, but I have no idea what to do to even get started. I don't have the money to get *my paws* on the perfect place I have in mind. Plus, I need to make money to live, so I'll probably keep doing the dog walking and house-sitting until I can get this idea flushed out. But I want to start tomorrow!"

"Yeah, I totally get that," chimes in **Andres**. "I've been 'inventing' gadgets for years. I went back and looked through my favs then settled on this electronic toy that can be controlled with a remote or app. Not sure what all is involved, but I'm ready to get started tomorrow too. First, I need to create the controller and have people test it. No way do I want to do sales or deal with pissed-off customers, so I need to figure out how to get this into people's hands through a third party. Maybe Amazon or retailers like Best Buy are good options."

Kaya is the last to share. "I've zoned in on providing assistance to elderly people who have mental and/or health challenges so they can stay in their homes safely. Depends on how quickly the software can be developed, but I'd like to start creating a business right away with the target of bringing on my first software client in three months. We might have to phase things in and start with contractors in homes. Then, as the software is developed, we'd roll into a more automated smart device service. I envision everything eventually being online and using cutting-edge technology."

"As you were sharing your ideas about each business, I could feel the enthusiasm and excitement but with twinges of apprehension. Not to worry!" I say enthusiastically. "Now we put on our detective hats to do some market sleuthing."

Assignment Prep: Market Research

"Next, we explore the competitive landscape looking for both direct and indirect competitors," I continue. "A direct competitor is one where you're going head-to-head with another business for customer dollars, like Coke versus Pepsi or McDonald's versus Burger King. An indirect competitor is in the same category or geographic space but offers something different than you. A simple way to think about it is a shopping mall with a food court. All the stores are competing for your attention and credit card but offer different options such as shoes, clothing, toys, electronics and entertainment. In the food court, all the restaurants are vying for your taste buds in a small compact space, so orange chicken is duking it out with cheeseburgers, pepperoni pizza and pulled pork barbecue.

"Let's bring it closer to home. Jade, to identify direct competitors, you need to find Asian fusion prepared food establishments operating in the geographic area you plan on covering in addition to those who attend events. Be sure to capture key identifiers such as location, delivery mechanism (e.g., food truck, delivery apps, restaurant), food type, price ranges, hours of operation, and unique promotions or setups.

"Next, make a second list of indirect competitors that are all types of fast-casual food providers in those same areas, because you're competing for the same discretionary meal dollars. Examples of those in your category are Mexican such as Chipotle, Taco Bell, Qdoba and On the Border; sandwich shops like Subway, Quiznos, Firehouse Subs, Jersey Mike's, Jimmy John's and grocery stores; Italian spots that include Olive Garden, Carrabba's, Maggiano's Buca di Beppo, Old Spaghetti Factory and little neighborhood restaurants; and pizza places such as local favorites, Pizza Hut, Little Caesars, Papa John's, Chunk E. Cheese, Sbarro and Dominos. You don't need to spend time on places like Chart House, Outback, Landry's and Ruth's Chris because those diners are looking for a different experience and expect to pay a significantly higher price.

"During your research, notice the 'Ad' links and general reference sites like Yelp (marketplaces that sell a bunch of what you're offering), and retail outlets and services that pop up on the first few pages of your competitive Google searches. You'll want to further explore how to get listed on these different platforms in the not-too-distant future when working on a marketing plan. By the way, I recommend using Google for all or most of your research since it's far and away the most popular search engine. Google has owned ninety-one percent market share over the last ten years, so you'll want to see what your potential customers see.[3] If you have extra time, check out where the links take you, places such as branded websites, third-party sites, resellers, affiliates, social media, Amazon, dead links and so on. Then take note of the search descriptions. Become aware of particular companies that keep showing up under different headlines and search words. It happens!

"The second step is to hypothesize the needs and wants of your potential customers. In Dylan's case, customers *aren't* everyone who owns a dog. Some people are lucky enough to stay at home with their pup and rarely, if ever, need someone else to walk or board it. You might find that those paying for dog services are owners who are single, travel for their jobs, live in high-rise buildings, have health issues or have families with young children. You'll further narrow that down to those people living within a limited geographic region or temporarily residing in an area close to where you'll provide services. This will help identify a potential customer pool.

"Lastly, brainstorm what you can offer prospective customers that they currently aren't getting. Andres, the toy industry is highly competitive, but every year, new products find success in niche markets. What new and exciting experiences could your toy offer kids in your target age range?

It doesn't have to be something brand new; instead, it could be a different way of combining common elements to create an experience that's uniquely your own."

I continue to address the concerns of all five budding entrepreneurs. "Be sure to do basic research online using websites, search engines, libraries, and startup-focused resources such as Service Corps of Retired Executives (SCORE) and the Small Business Administration.[4] You also might run across general business and industry resources, so capture those, too. For those with physical locations, drive around target areas, purchase competitors' offerings and attend potential customer events. Track your research in case you need additional details and help with future activities such as figuring out a marketing plan, pitching investors and recruiting partners/employees.

"Don't do the lazy Google search: typing in one or two different terms, looking only at the top ten entries for each and deciding you're the only person on the planet who has this idea," I advise. "Instead, brainstorm a list of terms and phrases people would use when looking for a solution like yours. Check them off as you go through them. Be sure to add any new ideas to your list as you delve deeper into your search.

"When you're doing this research, it's easy to get overwhelmed, dejected or feel like there's no opportunity. But stop yourself from going down that rabbit hole. Flip the narrative and see it as a *confirmation* of your idea, then focus on how your offer can fill a gap in the marketplace. This is where homing in on the ideal customer will help you crystallize your vision."

I look to see if they're taking this in. "I know this is a lot of detail, but it breaks down into three simple steps: identify direct and indirect competitors, figure out where your company fits, and determine the needs and wants of your potential customer pool.

"This is one of the creative steps, so be open to enlightenment. It's very important to do this all yourself or with business partners. Don't pay a high school kid twenty dollars to run eight or ten internet searches, then make up the rest. By slogging through this time-intensive process, you'll avoid spending that amount many times over in multiple pivots and marketing frustrations.

"Also, make note of trends and qualifiers," I emphasize. "Are fast-casual restaurants open only for lunch and dinner? Are the pet day cares only for dogs two years and up? Are in-home health services only offered in the ten largest U.S cities? If you make any assumptions to narrow down and focus your research, capture those for future reference. If you're doing it right, this will take more than a couple of distracted hours while bingeing on your favorite reality show, so plan accordingly.

"To clarify your assignment for the next meeting, identify direct and indirect competitors either by name or descriptive category. Then paint an overall picture of the needs and wants these businesses address for their customers. Also, list any needs that aren't being met but for which you could provide a solution. Summarize your lists on a poster so we can all see what you found out; this will aid in our discussions and idea generation. Finally, share how what you learned further defines your niche opportunity in the marketplace."

ASSIGNMENT 3
Research to Find Your Market Opportunity

1) Identify your direct (companies with similar offers) and indirect (businesses in the same general category but that provide different products or services) competitors individually, by grouping or by descriptive category.

2) Create a list of needs and wants businesses like yours address for their customers. If you see any needs that aren't being addressed that your business could pursue, add those, too. Put these in a summary poster to discuss in the next meeting.

3) Brainstorm ideas of things you can offer to carve out a niche in the marketplace. Tracking these in a spreadsheet or creating multiple lists is a good approach so you can add information in categories as you come across it in your research.

Following Your Niche

As the energetic entrepreneurs arrive, I ask that they display their posters on the easels distributed around the room. During the session, each person will share their research results with the group to gather feedback along with suggested additions, deletions or changes.

I start by saying, "I hope you gained new insights into your unique market space and that you're feeling good about the direction of your business idea. It's not necessary to have every little detail figured out yet, but you should be crystallizing the vision of what you'll deliver to the outside world.

"Let's go around the room so you can each share any updates to your business scope and direction. Also, identify direct and indirect competitors, describe the needs and wants of your potential target customers, and tell us about any new product or service ideas you landed on."

"I'll start," says **Malik**, who wants to provide engineering management services on a project basis. "Wow! There are a lot of contractors and outsourcing companies out there. Instead of listing all the companies, I grouped them based on commonalities such as size, industry, or function. On another sheet, I specifically identified those focused on smaller opportunities in my particular area of expertise to do a deeper dive later. Also, I asked for feedback from colleagues and potential clients on my business idea. I wanted to know what areas were hard for them to find time for or qualified people to address. Doing this allowed me to focus on short-term project management gigs like helping clients who are temporarily short-staffed, have people out on leave, or only need technical help for a single project or several small projects."

ENGINEERING MANAGEMENT SERVICES

MALIK

CUSTOMER NEEDS/WANTS

- Temporary expertise for a project
- Reduce employee overhead costs
- Coverage for employees on temporary leave
- Contractors looking for subcontractors

DIRECT COMPETITORS

- Online project contractors (Vetted, Guru, and other sites)
- In-house resources at medium to large companies (task forces, Agile groups, other project teams)
- Group of small-sized industry contractors in the region
- Several independent contractors from LinkedIn network with similar experience

INDIRECT COMPETITORS

- 7,750 technology engineering companies nationally
- National contract technology placement companies
- National / international project outsourcing companies
- Artificial Intelligence (AI) and machine learning solutions

"It's great how you've quickly shifted from an interim gig mindset to jumping into full-fledged entrepreneur mode with both feet," I point out. "I'm not sure if you're aware of the rideshare industry's fight with various government entities about driver classification. They have been categorized as contractors by companies like Lyft and Uber, thus avoiding the additional costs and obligations associated with employees. However, what they require of drivers could be classified as employee-type directives as defined by regulatory entities. Worker advocates and the rideshare industry have been, and still are, battling over this issue.

"Companies are constantly grappling with decisions regarding worker versus contractor classifications, overseas outsourcing and various types of visa hires like H-1B for specialty occupations, especially in the tech industry. It seems there's an opportunity to help small to medium-sized businesses understand and manage these issues. Instead of trying to compete on the same level as nationally recognized industry leaders, Malik, you could devise a cost-effective, headache-free solution," I suggest.

"You're right," he responds. "That's a big thorny issue from both the employee and company perspective. Instead of just contracting out qualified warm bodies, I could provide the reporting, management and tracking side, too, and charge additional fees."

"Absolutely!" I say wholeheartedly. "You could position your business as added insurance and protection against a risk they might not have understood existed. Instead of competing against online outsourcing giants, you're acting as a trusted partner and providing a more customized solution.

Certainly something to consider as we move along through the process. Who's next?"

Jade chimes in. "I did the same, grouping competitors because so many food options exist. Plus, it was hard to get too detailed about customer needs with the multiple factors involved when people are deciding what to eat. My focus is on quality food made quickly that tastes good with a variety of flavors. From there, I thought about why people would want that meal option. All that brain stress led to hours of mulling over what my niche could be. In the food business, it's all about being in the right location — whether that's a stand-alone brick-and-mortar restaurant, a shared kitchen space with delivery apps, a food truck, a pop-up event booth or a food court setup. The flexibility and low startup costs of a shared commissary kitchen with app-only delivery stood out as the safest, quickest, and cheapest way for me to get started."

FOOD SERVICES

JADE

CUSTOMER NEEDS/WANTS

- Quick and healthy take-home meals customized for a variety of dietary restrictions
- Family meals with a variety of flavor options in one stop
- Affordable, healthy, tasty and quickly-prepared food for individuals
- Flavorful meals that can be ordered using popular delivery apps
- Catered meals with varied dietary options for groups or meetings

DIRECT COMPETITORS

- Approximately 140 Asian fusion-style restaurants in the county (some are franchises with multiple locations)
- Approximately 320 barbecue-type restaurants in the county (some are franchises with multiple locations)
- Estimate 35 commissary or shared kitchens in the county, and it's unknown how many use delivery apps

INDIRECT COMPETITORS

- Approximately 500 mobile carts and food trucks offering various cuisine in the county
- Estimate 13,000 fast-food and fast-casual restaurants in the county
- Dozens of food providers participate in each large special event (e.g., county fairs, music festivals, holiday celebrations)
- Meal kits shipped to homes pre-made

"You've made some great progress, Jade," I say encouragingly. "I know startup costs are a concern, but if you feel strongly about an opportunity, there are multiple ways to get funding. Please don't throw away your dream of a physical space just yet. Also, if you decide to go with the food truck, then that group would move from an indirect competitor to direct. There are only so many trucks that can physically fit into the prime revenue events or locations. This type of crowded market provides a good opportunity for cooperative competition or *co-opetition*. That's when competitive businesses turn into partners usually for a product, service, project or event. For example, you might want to pool your efforts and resources with salad or dessert trucks at events to offer a complete sidewalk meal while saving on costs."

"That's an interesting twist," replies Jade. "It would be great to work with experienced food truckers to help me learn the ropes."

Dylan pipes up next. "Okay, I want to go next! I knew there were a bunch of dog-walking, boarding and grooming places, but all the options are crazy! I still think a bougie place for pets and owners would be popular for people who want a vacation experience with their fur babies every day of the week. There seem to be a ton of dog-walking and boarding companies, and random people doing those things, so I want to create a unique experience. My vision is to have a place where dogs and pet parents are pampered — like a country club for humans and their furry friends. So, here are my lists. Oh, and Malik added *pet tech* under indirect competitors before we started today so I don't have more detail yet on that one."

BOUGIE PET PLACE

DYLAN

CUSTOMER NEEDS/WANTS

- Connecting with and getting updates on pet when away from home
- Relieving guilt over not spending enough time with pet
- Status symbol by giving pet pampered experiences
- Improved sense of self-worth by having a healthy pet
- Having peace of mind when traveling or needing someone to look after a pet
- Time savings

DIRECT COMPETITORS

- Brick-and-mortar pet care locations – 73 in the metro area
- Individuals (local kids, neighbors, friends, etc.)
- Veterinarians and dog walkers – estimate 150 in the metro area
- Gig people found on apps (e.g., Rover and Wag!)

INDIRECT COMPETITORS

- Mobile grooming services – only found 3 locally
- Human spas and retreats that cater to pet owners in the U.S. – too time consuming to count individually due to variety
- Approximately 32,000 dog-walking companies in the U.S.
- Pet-friendly hotels that allow four-legged friends
- High-tech home gadgets for pet engagement, training, and monitoring

"This sounds fantastic, Dylan," I state. "The challenge for you is to figure out a pricing strategy that will turn a profit so you can stay in business over the long haul, given the wide range of competitive options. Will you charge a membership fee and, if so, what does that cover? Will people be able to buy daily, weekly or monthly passes? What types of optional services will be offered? Will you allow walk-ins and, if so, what is that pricing? How many customers do you need to purchase the various tiered offers to cover your costs?" A helpless look followed by one of dread washed over Dylan's face. "Don't worry, we'll work through how to understand financials as we continue through the process," I say reassuringly.

Andres jumps in next. "Before digging around, I didn't really have a clear idea about how the final version of the toy would work. I just knew that what I created was rad to play with. After doing the research, I'm blown away by the sheer number of toys and all the different specialty areas targeted by age group. Plus, integrating with the internet or an app seems to be more of an obstacle than an added fun feature. Anyway, I've decided to create a toy in the STEAM category — an educational approach that incorporates the arts into the more-familiar STEM model, which includes science, technology, engineering and mathematics — for older kids to build weird worlds created from 3-D images they design. When ordering, customers step through various options to create their unique fantastical universe. Then the toy is delivered in puzzle-type pieces for the kid to put together. It would either turn out like the original design or be a completely new one. I'm still working through details but was able to do some research."

STEAM TOY

ANDRES

CUSTOMER NEEDS/WANTS

- Intellectual development through play
- Family engagement and bonding
- Entertainment and enjoyment with friends
- Pride in owning the coolest and hottest new toy

DIRECT COMPETITORS

- Amazon search lists 1,000+ STEAM toys for ages 8-13
- Building sets for ages 18 and under is estimated at 350
- Unknown number of 3-D printers with software to create own toys and designs

INDIRECT COMPETITORS

- Top global competitors with multiple iconic brands: Playmobil, Nintendo, Mattel, Lego, Hasbro, Disney
- 100s of traditional toy lines (Barbie, Legos, Hot Wheels)
- Electronic games where kids interact and compete online

"Andres," I respond, "it's obviously a competitive marketplace. One of the most important things to do when building out something new is to get feedback from users along the way. Since you don't have a working prototype yet, start by observing kids in your age group playing with available toys similar to what you have envisioned. Give them several options and don't intervene — only observe and note what activities and challenges keep their interest. Cycle through these testing groups during the development phase before you invest a ton of money in live production.

"Your toy will never be a perfect fit for everyone. But when you get it to a point that users keep playing with it and want to share with their friends, then that's your cue to roll it out."

Andres asks, "Where do I find these kids, and do I need their parents' permission?"

"You can start with family and friends, but whoever they are, be sure to have both the parents and kids sign a waiver in case any issues arise and especially if you plan on filming anything for research." I advise. "You could also reach out to STEAM teachers, groups or hobby organizations to see if they would be willing to help. As development moves along, working with testing labs could be useful, plus you'll want to pass a safety inspection test before releasing your toy to the public. A testing lab can provide that."

"Looks like it's my turn," observes **Kaya**. "Since I've been in the health care industry for most of my professional career, I didn't find many surprises when investigating in-home elder care options. What I did discover were many options for different levels of care, and those choices have people cobbling together solutions to meet their needs. Given time, money and resource constraints, figuring out the best move puts stress on families. This exercise made me realize what a complex decision health care is and how challenging all the options are to navigate."

"Kaya, I know this is a challenge for many families, so there's definitely an opportunity in the space if you can find the right balance between quality of care and cost." I say reassuringly. "Next, you need to drill down on what type of care your business will offer, the logistics to get there, staffing and a sweet spot in the marketplace."

HOME HEALTH CARE

KAYA

CUSTOMER NEEDS/WANTS

- Peace of mind by having a trusted solution
- High level of health care knowledge for in-home solution
- Time and resources to provide suitable care
- Quality care at affordable prices and help navigating the health care ecosystem
- Personalized care to address unique needs
- Remote monitoring capability and notifications

DIRECT COMPETITORS

- Friends and family support providing help with care
- Local in-home medical care services (difficult to quantify)
- Independent local nurses or caretakers
- Several large health care provider marketplaces like Care.com and Caring.com

INDIRECT COMPETITORS

- Private elder care facilities
- Monitoring and video medical support
- Veterans Administration (VA) facilities with various levels of eligibility and care
- 17,500+ federal and state-supported nursing homes in California

Before giving the next assignment, I say, "Great job, everyone! Once you start talking to prospects and bringing on customers, find out how they learned about your company and what drove their purchase decisions. Baking in a feedback loop into your business operations from the start will give you an edge against your competitor."

Assignment Prep:
Find Your Evangelists

I prepare the group for the assignment. "Now, take that list of customer needs and wants, figure out which one(s) your business will address, and get a clear picture of the type of people who'd be most excited to use your new product or service. Your company *evangelists* will emerge out of this niche group — the early adopters willing to spread the word. They're excited to try something new, willing to give feedback, and glad to be the 'go-to experts' who know the ins and outs of the newest thing. Mostly, they enjoy sharing their knowledge and experiences with others."

"Okay, that's nice in theory, but how do we figure out the niche market, who the early adopters are and how to find them?" Jade asks. "I think of my neighbor, Sherry, and my co-worker, Hakim, as potential early customers, but they're nothing alike. So how do I figure out the commonality to find others like them?"

"It's the entrepreneur's Holy Grail, forever chased but never fully grasped," I respond. "People, competition and our world are constantly shifting like a cat trying to capture the zigzagging laser dot. Sometimes companies think they have a solution for one problem, but people end up using it to address a completely different one. In other instances, a major change in the international theater like Russia's invasion of Ukraine or worldwide shutdowns in response to COVID-19 can have an almost immediate impact on people's purchases. The best way to approach finding your evangelists is to make assumptions, test them, track the results, adjust as needed and then start the cycle all over again. It's important to always be *listening* to your customers through their words and actions while also paying attention to what's happening that might impact your customers and business.

"In your case, Jade, the first step is to profile your flavor fans, then figure out the best way to deliver your scrumptious meals to them. Start by looking at the lists on your poster and make an educated guess about what type of person will buy the food you want to prepare in the time frame, geographic location, environment and quantity that you're considering. Are they single business professionals, families, students or some other demographically definable group? Or does it make more sense to target people who have an activity in common like country music aficionados, keto dieters, road bike enthusiasts, farmers' market regulars or fine dining enthusiasts? It could be a combination of both approaches.

"Once you've defined your target group, then figure out where they congregate and the best way to reach them. Maybe you decide on college students, so start looking into how on-campus dining facilities operate. If professionals in business parks sound like an opportunity, a food truck could be a great option.

"I've listed several questions on the board to get the wheels turning on how to identify your niche market and early adopters.

Will this product or service be used by individuals, families, groups, businesses, nonprofits, governments or other target groups?

"The first one asks you to determine who will use your product or service. Malik, a good starting point for you is to ask, 'Is my best opportunity focusing on app developers, network providers, private universities, city governments, military branches or something else?' Then keep drilling down until you find the sweet spot. Keep in mind, this first cut applies to where you focus your efforts when starting out, but that could quickly expand or shift based on feedback and results."

Are there common demographics that stand out such as gender, age group or residence?

"Second, capture any easily identifiable demographics. For example, Kaya, decision makers for the elderly include adult children who typically in the forty to sixty-year-old age range. And Dylan, this is a natural question if you're targeting doggy pet parents in a specific geographic area. We know people will only drive so far to drop off their fur babies, so you probably have a limited geographic range. Unless you decide to create a destination retreat experience, then that's a different approach."

Do people in your target community have a shared hobby or interest?

"Next, do your target customers have common interests or hobbies? Andres, your general focus will be on middle school kids who have an interest in STEAM activities, competitions and events. Could you drill down further and target kids who are Star Wars fans or play Lumino City?"

Are there specific places or events where your product or service would be highly desired?

"Look at specific places where potential customers congregate. Jade, festivals and other outdoor events that create space for food trucks to enhance the experience could be possible targets for you. Or, if you stick with the app only-approach, there will be a limited geographic area where your food can be feasibly delivered."

Do environmental factors such as weather or internet speed affect the use of your product?

"Are there environmental factors to consider? This also applies to your business concept, Jade. People are likely to go outside and wait for their order to be prepared at a food truck during the warm months. For you, Kaya, high-speed, reliable internet access could be a requirement for your health-monitoring solutions."

Are there specific activities potential customers tend to engage in?

"Also look at the activities, principles or regulations guiding buyers. Malik, it might be a good idea to target software and app companies that have regular product releases or mid-sized network companies offering compensation packages that include generous time off, such as maternity/paternity leave or sabbaticals. Dylan, your potential clients might shop at specific stores and malls or travel to posh vacation spots."

Would the purchase be driven by certain events (e.g., holidays, sporting events, religious activities, graduations)?

"Be sure to look at holidays and events that might spike purchases. Andres, this fits in nicely with your toy concept. Probably the biggest sales opportunity is around the Christmas holiday, but there might be other large STEAM-related events like conventions and competitions, too."

Is your product or service normally purchased as a gift or for personal use? If it's a gift, then who is the actual buyer?

"Lastly, do people buy your product or service as a gift? Dylan, this could be something worth exploring. Will all your sales be to pet owners? Or is a spa gift card something special and unique that people would buy? This is also a question for

Andres. Do kids decide they want the toy and the parents purchase it? Do kids purchase toys with their own money? And Malik, will you contract directly with hiring companies or with third-party aggregators? For all of you, it's important to identify the various buyer scenarios of your product or service," I emphasize.

"When starting out, your goal is to figure out a *niche group* to zero in on and focus your efforts there. If you can identify another group that might be just as valuable but can't decide between them, then start with both groups. Gather feedback as quickly as possible. I suggest you put one on the back burner when first launching unless you have the processes and resources to pursue both.

"Share your targeted group in our next meeting and come with a detailed description of what this niche market looks like. Make sure it's complete with descriptors and behaviors that will help identify your potential customers. For example, Dylan's pet services could target busy single professionals who own medium and large dog breeds. They're outdoorsy, enjoy traveling and live in a specific geolocation. Your goal is to avoid saying 'everyone and their mothers could use it' and start identifying 'a targeted few who will become hardcore fans.'"

Feeling a bit confused, Malik asks, "What if I sell to businesses that have a gatekeeper, a budget approver and multiple decision-makers? How do I figure out details about all those people and keep them straight in my head?"

"Malik, providing services to other businesses — commonly referred to as B-to-B or B2B — can be challenging depending on the size of the organization," I explain. "Typically, small businesses buy in ways similar to consumers, so you would define your niche mostly based on the owners' or decision makers' profile.

"With mid- to large-sized companies, it's helpful to find a champion inside the organization who believes in you and will help guide you through the internal maze. Also, identify the typical job titles involved in the purchase process. If you're providing project management solutions, the champion might be a director of product management or engineering with the vice president holding sign-off authority. Create general descriptors for each of the key people involved in the purchase decision. It might also help to lay out a flowchart identifying the process and level of influence everyone holds. A quick nugget: Nobody wants to look foolish, so conveying trust and reliability is always going to be important.

"Some organizations, like federal contractors and government entities, will use a Request for Proposal, commonly referred to as RFP, or a similarly-named process for purchasing. Typically posted publicly, these RFPs have strict deadlines and submission requirements.

"To summarize the B-to-B market approach, your first step is to determine the size and type of business you're targeting. After that, identify the purchasing process; define who within the organization is likely to influence or make the buying decision for your solution, and craft a sales approach based on the information available."

"Each company has different titles, processes, and reporting structures," Malik says worriedly. "How do I figure out what works across multiple companies?"

"I'm guessing you'll be starting out small, so identify specific companies that you're familiar with and/or have contacts inside," I reply. "Use LinkedIn to figure out who can help you within targeted companies and a customer management solution like Salesforce, Sugar CRM or Zoho to keep track of all the contacts. Also, attending networking and industry events will help you find opportunities outside your professional sphere.

"You have a lot of educated guessing to do when describing your niche market and early adopters for our next meeting. Remember, this is your first cut at determining your target market. There will be lots of twists and turns once you get real-life feedback, but for now, put a stake in the ground that will move you forward."

ASSIGNMENT 4
Identify Niche Market and Customer Descriptors

1) What are the commonalities or traits of your likely early adopters? Who would derive value from what you have to offer? What do they have in common? Come up with as much detail as possible to describe your niche market using geography, demographics and behavioral attributes.

2) Is the person who normally makes the buying decision different than the one who will use or consume your product or service? If so:

    a. Describe the user or consumer of the good or service.

    b. Describe who makes the buying decision and why.

    c. Describe any additional purchase influencer(s).

Finding Customers in a Haystack

"**I**t may not seem like it, but we're making progress," I say to get our next meeting started. "So, to recap, your assignment was to identify your niche market along with characteristics and behaviors that describe the early adopters. Think about people who would be most excited to use what you offer and key descriptors that distinguish them from random people on the street.

"Keep in mind, this is a starting point. As you interact with customers, you'll learn more about where your business fits and who your real fans are, so these descriptors will likely morph over time."

"I'll kick us off," **Andres** jumps in. "After switching up and learning more about tweens, it seemed easier to reach techie kids based on their activities and the other toys they play with. Parents will probably be the ones paying for this toy, but the best way to reach them is through their kids – especially those who are curious. I came up with the following descriptors for my early adopters.

Andres – Early Adopters

- Kids between nine to thirteen years old who enjoy puzzles, Legos, building sets and/or models
- Students in STEAM classes, attending camps or participating in competitions
- Families owning two or more computers, tablets and/or smartphones with internet access
- Households with total incomes of $95,000 or more that can afford to buy new expensive, interactive toys

"Those are great descriptors, Andres," I say. "The next step is to dig deeper by talking to parents and kids about your idea. If you have a minimum viable product, also called MVP, which is a basic working toy without all the bells and whistles you envisioned, let kids play with it. Notice what breaks and when they lose interest, adjust and move forward. All right, who wants to go next?"

"I will," states **Kaya**. "Two groups make decisions about elder care: the caregiving family and the older adult in need of a health solution. The decisions could be made in advance or when an immediate solution is needed. I feel that, ultimately, elder care is a family decision, so I need to focus on both the caregivers and elderly patients. Here are my early adopter descriptors.

Kaya – Early Adopters

- Adult children with a parent or parents facing physical or mental degradation to the point of being unsafe to stay alone
- Those who can afford $3.000-$10,000 a month for in-home medical support (will be more specific once pricing is finalized)
- Geographically located in San Diego County and Orange County areas of Southern California
- Adult caregivers comfortable with technology who have a smartphone and/or are connected to the internet via a computer
- Adult children who struggle with full-time caregiving because they work and/or have children at home

"Good job, Kaya," I say. "You might have additional technology requirements that can help narrow your focus if that becomes a big part of your offerings. I also suggest looking into various ways people can pay for your services such as special insurance, Medicare/Medicaid or workers' compensation. Researching this will help you identify those who can afford your solutions."

"Okay, I'll go next," says **Dylan**. "I'm focused on building a clientele that will eventually want to socialize with dog owners or drop off their pups at a bougie doggy establishment.

It will have an area where humans can hang out and meet each other while pets do their thing. Interactive daycare, spa services, training, grooming and long-term boarding will be on the menu. Here are the people who would be interested.

Dylan – Early Adopters

- Busy professionals who own dogs
- Working adults who make $85,000 or more annually and live in the San Diego area near downtown
- Those who travel for work or leisure five or more times a year
- Dog parents who purchase fresh and healthy pet foods
- Owners who use technology to entertain and/or monitor their dogs at home

"I can envision your clientele right now, Dylan," I comment. "The only descriptor I'd question is annual income. Is that for a family, household or individual? It might be a bit arbitrary. Maybe focus on other things they might buy such as the healthy dog foods you mentioned. For example, would Chewy subscribers be a good fit? Also, think about high-end brands they might buy for themselves such as Nike, Gucci or North Face, or consider specific apps they may use related to dating or dog ownership."

"Oh, I get it," Dylan responds. "I should think about what other things my potential clients might buy to find them."

"I went down that path," comments **Jade**. "This was a difficult exercise figuring out more detail on potential customers beyond 'San Diegans who like Asian and barbecue food.' They could be anyone, anywhere. So, I narrowed it down to 'people looking for a tasty, healthy, fast casual option for lunch or dinner.' It seems like focusing on locations and activities versus demographic information is what I need to do next. I decided to go with the food truck delivery option instead of the app-only, so we'll target the following:

Jade – Early Adopters

- Summer weekends at Balboa Park and other popular tourist areas within a one-hour drive
- People who enjoy watching the Food Network, cooking competitions and tasting new dishes
- Office park locations during work hours with few to no food options within walking distance
- Potential special events such as large balloon festivals, county fairs, and outdoor food and wine festivals

"Those are all good ideas," I say. "With a food truck, your options will be narrowed down by licensing restrictions, event entry costs, availability, accessibility and timing. Is there any particular diet or lifestyle that would be a natural fit with your food? For example, country music fans, distance runners, museum patrons, hot sauce lovers or craft beer drinkers. There might be many types who could find something they like in your truck, but a select group might fall in love with most of your menu items and keep coming back for more. Work on that to focus in on your messaging, Jade. Next?"

"Since I provide services to businesses," states **Malik**. "I initially thought I could just call businesspeople I've worked with in the past and get projects, but maybe I need a little more diligence. From my experience, most directors inside big companies have control of a budget and could sign off on contracts of my dollar size. To grow and go after bigger projects, I'll probably need support at the VP level. For now, I'm focused on these organizational aspects.

Malik – Early Adopters

- Technology companies that provide services to businesses and consumers
- Mid-sized and large companies with personal connections (to avoid drawn-out RFP situations)
- California-based companies, or potentially other tech hub cities like Austin, D.C., Seattle and Boston
- International locations are an option in places like London, Frankfurt, Tokyo and Hong Kong
- Managers responsible for user interface and user experience design and analysis for new product releases, or groups responsible for life cycle product updates

"Malik, I like your idea of targeting mid-sized tech companies because they tend to have fewer internal resources and a less arduous purchasing decision process," I respond. "When talking with contacts, be explicit about what you're looking for in a project. Make it easy for people to think of specific opportunities. Also, you might focus on either consumer or business projects to start. That's because of a natural delineation in product development processes, even though you might have done both. My guess is you prefer one over the other, so go in the direction of your preference to bring out your natural enthusiasm."

Assignment Prep: Own Your Niche

I explain the group's next steps. "Now that you know *what* you want to offer and *who* you plan on selling to, the next step is figuring out *how* to carve out a niche in the marketplace — in other words, what's the vision for your company? Address these questions: *How is your product or service different than what's already available, and how does it compel someone to change what they're doing today?* Your answers could be based on any number of things such as more convenient proximity, easier to use, uniqueness, a new twist on an old way of doing things or simplifying someone's life.

"Remember, this is your starting point. Validating your business assumptions and clearly identifying your core customers will happen over time. Be creative, understand what business you're really in, and focus in on your intention — that is, *how do you want people to feel after purchasing and using your product or service?* Perhaps they feel relief or even smart, content, proud, excited or a multitude of emotions. Oprah Winfrey suggests you consider what your intention is before undertaking a major project or change in your life. [5]

"Your homework for the next meeting is to articulate your company vision and succinctly describe your business niche: *How is your offering different from that of your competitors?* This is often referred to as a Unique Selling Proposition, or USP. To help you work through this exercise, here are some questions to ask yourselves:

Unique Selling Proposition

- Why would people search for what I have to offer?
- What will I provide that's unique (e.g., geographical location, type of community served, industry solution, specialized interests)?
- What does company success look like beyond turning a profit?
- How will the world benefit if the company is successful?
- How will people engage with the company and consume what's offered?
- How does interacting with the company make people feel?

"Next, create a clear, concise vision statement that inspires you and will become the underpinnings of decision-making and actions within your business for the long haul. Your USP explains to people where your business fits in the world. In one or two sentences, it should concisely state what your company provides to customers that they can't get anywhere else.

"One of the best examples of creating a simple and extremely effective vision statement is Southwest Airlines.

Every decision made and action taken from the executive suite to gate attendants is driven by the company vision. It's been more than fifty years since Rollin King drew out 'The Texas Triangle' route on a cocktail napkin, sharing his dream of a short-haul intrastate carrier with friend and attorney Herb Kelleher, and his passion still guides the company today.[6] When opportunities or challenges are presented, they should be examined through vision-statement-glasses to determine the best course of action and help the business stay on course.[7]

Southwest Airlines' Vision

To be the world's most loved, most efficient, and most profitable airline.

Southwest Airlines' Purpose (USP)

Connect people to what's important in their lives through friendly, reliable, and low-cost air travel.

"As you can see the vision is simple, precise and presents an easy-to-understand idea. The purpose provides direction on how to support and execute the vision. Go back and review all the work you've done to this point for ideas and clarity," I suggest. "This is where your startup dream meets real-world action."

ASSIGNMENT 5
Create a Company Vision and USP

1. Articulate the essence of your company's reason for being by creating a short, succinct vision statement.
2. Describe how your offering differs from your competitors' offering — your Unique Selling Proposition.

Chapter 6

Mapping Out the Future

I start our next session with this question: "How did it go developing your company vision and USP? Also, how is everyone feeling so far?"

Dylan excitedly states, "I'm *so* into this planning thing! It's helping me see that my big dream can come true!"

"Same here!" **Kaya** concurs. "I feel like I'm really getting back to my roots and remembering what's important. Also, this process is reinforcing my decision to start a health care company and not just to find a way to escape a frustrating career. It has me truly believing I can have a positive impact on people's lives. That's why I got into the field to begin with. It's exciting and scary at the same time."

Confesses **Andres**, "For me, designing things is dope, but I still have doubts I can make money with these creations. I'm struggling a bit with everything required to make it happen."

"First, I applaud all of you for putting in the work to get this far," I praise. "Many people don't think this kind of background effort is valuable, but I know it will pay off in spades down the road. Keep pushing through, Andres. The process is working for all of you so keep pushing forward. I'm sure you all have many unanswered questions, but we're almost through the blueprint and foundation phases, and moving into putting up drywall and hammering the nails. Okay, let's hear what everyone came up with."

"I want to go first!" exclaims **Dylan**. "What I figured out through my many jobs is that most pet parents think of their animals as part of the family, and having fur babies makes it super easy to meet other people. I want to create a place where it all comes together, so I've made a few changes after the last meeting. Here goes:

"My **vision** for the company is to *create pampering and nurturing experiences for humans and their pets*. The **USP** is to *provide personalized, pampered care by understanding preferences, needs and personalities to create a positive, safe community where pets and people want to gather*."

"That sounds great, Dylan. To make the USP more impactful and succinct, take out the "by" section because that's execution detail you don't need. I'm looking forward to seeing where you take this business."

Dylan – Final Vision & USP

Vision:
Create pampering and nurturing experiences for humans and their pets.

USP:
Provide personalized, stylish environments to create a positive, safe community where pets and people want to gather.

Kaya interjects. "I'll go next. I'm passionate about helping people, but it's been a challenge figuring out how to be different than all of the other providers out there coupled with staffing concerns. I was talking to my friend and ex-colleague Josh, who is a nutritionist. We've decided to work together on a new concept. Instead of only providing in-home care, we want to give clients drug-free options to health problems by analyzing and improving their lifestyle, nutrition, and home and work environments," she says. "Josh and I worked through the vision statement and came up with this:

"The **vision** is: *Advise and educate people on how to live a healthier life through nutrition, lifestyle and environmental management.* The **USP** is: *Bring together all the facets that affect well-being and prescribe healthy natural solutions as opposed to drug-centric health management. We evaluate clients' lives by looking at all the environments they're exposed to, demands on their time, budget and accessibility to solutions.*"

"Congrats, Kaya," I say. "It's exciting to be moving forward with a partner, and it sounds like you're more passionate about this shift in direction than before. Many opportunities exist in this space as our health care system deals with complex issues like sporadic pandemic threats, cost management, affordability and insurance regulations. One suggestion, though," I offer. "Consider deleting that last sentence in your USP, because it's more of an execution statement rather than a clean strategic differentiator. Also, if you modify the first sentence to read something like 'Bring together all the facets that affect mental, emotional and physical well-being through healthy natural lifestyle solutions and environmental management,' then it's a stronger USP statement."

Kaya – Final Vision & USP

Vision:

Advise and educate people on how to live a healthier life through nutrition, lifestyle and environmental management.

USP:

Evaluate and modify all the facets that affect mental, emotional and physical well-being through education and behavior modification.

"I'll go next," says **Malik**. "As a detail person, I've been focused on getting this consulting business off the ground, so shifting to this 'pie-in-the-sky fluffy stuff' is a challenge for me. Plus, I'm still not sure if this is something I want to do long-term or just for a while until another opportunity comes along. Anyway, here's how I took a shot at this assignment:

My **vision** is to *offer personalized engineering services that combine customer analysis with technical implementation.* For the **USP,** I came up with this customer-first approach to engineering solutions: *Understand client challenges and business outcomes before developing recommended actions and implementing best practices to ensure solutions are integrated successfully."*

I respond with, "For a different perspective, think about creating a solid vision statement as having an out-of-body experience. Imagine yourself floating over your business one, five, and ten years from now. *What current of purpose do you want to see flowing across all the twists and turns over time?* That becomes the catalyst for your business. Using this approach, let's rethink your vision statement, Malik."

A group discussion ensues, giving him lots of ideas to work with. Malik summarizes the discussion by saying, "Okay, my new vision statement is this: *Be a catalyst for business transformation by conducting personalized client analyses and developing customized solutions."*

Malik – Final Vision & USP

Vision:

Enable business transformation through
innovation and optimization of technology and
processes.

USP:

Understand client challenges and business
outcomes to ensure customized solutions are
integrated seamlessly.

Jade then takes center stage. "I want to start this business because of my love of creative cooking, so I tried to convey it in my vision statement," she states. My **vision** is to *create fast, fresh unique food for busy people delivered where and when they want it.* My **USP** comes from experimenting with many nontraditional flavors, which will give me an edge against other food truck vendors. It states to *craft unique flavors by combining different spices, foods and cooking techniques to create a healthy fast-food experience.*"

"Sounds good, Jade, but I'd make a couple of changes," I suggest. "I think you have more passion than is stated in your vision. Also, aren't all food trucks in the fast-food business? So, is that really a differentiator? And don't many other food trucks provide unique flavors?"

"Yes, all food trucks essentially provide fast food, but if I move into a brick-and-mortar location, I still want to provide fast/casual food," Jade replies. "Now that I'm saying that, maybe I should change the vision to *create flavorful comfort food with a twist inspired by healthy eating and respect for the earth.*"

"That sounds like a better fit," I say. "What about the USP?"

Jade rattles off, "*Inspired by the zest of barbecue and flavor of Asian spices, we create unique flavor experiences that surprise the palate and warm the heart.*"

"Sounds fantastic!" I exclaim. "I like how it captures your origin story of barbecue and Asian food but doesn't limit where you take your unique epicurean imagination."

Jade – Final Vision & USP

Vision:

Create healthy flavorful comfort food with a twist
while respecting the earth.

USP:

Deliver unique tasty experiences that surprise
the palate and warm the heart inspired by the
zest of barbecue and flavor of Asian Spices.

"Okay, Andres, what do you have to share?"

"Since I'm focused on creating interesting stuff, my vision and USP lean toward *what I want to do* versus *where the business might go*," says **Andres**. My **vision** is to *entertain kids, young and old, with interactive toys that educate and engage.* That leads to a **USP** of *creating engaging STEAM-focused interactive toys that can be customized to educate and entertain kids within targeted age groups. Personalized creations can be shared and interchanged with others.*"

"Andres, I like the vision," I say, "but I have a clarification question. Do you want to focus more on the needs and wants of targeted age groups or more on toy innovation? If it's the creative side, then you probably want to remove the reference to age groups and possibly STEAM."

"Yeah, I see what you mean," responds Andres. "Let's try this USP: *Create engaging, unique, interactive toys and puzzles that can be customized and interchanged to feed the imagination.*"

"That's much better," I say. "It allows for more innovation and isn't constrained to one group. I also really like the focus on feeding people's imaginations. It sums up perfectly what your business can be. Based on the change in your vision statement, you probably should change out *toys* for *gadgets* or some other more general descriptor.

Andres – Final Vision & USP

Vision:
Entertain kids, young and old, with interactive engaging inventions that challenge the intellect.

USP:
Create unique, interactive devices and puzzles that can be customized to feed the imagination.

"As we continue through the process and if any of you decide to shift, then go ahead and adjust your USP to reflect the change."

Andres responds, "That brings up some things that have me worried. How do I make this into a successful business without an MBA or real-world management experience? How do I determine if I need to bring on a partner, get a loan or use contractors like Malik to get my toy made?"

"Those are great questions, Andres, and we'll touch on all those concerns," I reply. "It's also a great segue into the organizational phase of the process."

Assignment Prep:
Organizational Plans

Next, I introduce planning as the group's next step. "For the next meeting, think about how you want your company to operate, where you want it to go long-term and what your exit strategy will be. This will affect your funding options, legal tactics, growth direction and more, so take time to think about what type of culture you want to create and work in every day."

I draw their attention to a poster of startup statistics.[8,9]

Interesting Startup Stats

Often new entrepreneurs think their challenges and choices are unique, so it helps to realize many have walked similar paths.

Percentage of entrepreneurs that have put some money in their new business	**89%**[*]
Number of new businesses started by first-time entrepreneurs	**1/3**[*]
Number of businesses started out of the home	**69%**[*]
Number of businesses initially funded with less than $5,000	**1/3**[*]
Additional capital companies with two founders raise	**30%**[**]

[*]Startup Statistics 2023 - The Numbers You Need to Know
[**]Raising Capital for Startups: 8 Statistics That Will Surprise You

"Quick question: Are the startups out of people's homes mostly certain types of businesses like Malik's consulting?" asks Andres.

"Most would guess that, but in fact, only 33% fall into that category," I reply. "The rest are in the consumer sector and natural resources. Technology has provided the tools for many types of businesses to start in a spare room or garage.[10] Great question. Okay, back to determining your organization type. The first step is to decide if you'll be starting the business by yourself, with a partner or as a group. It doesn't mean you can't evolve later as your business needs change, but consider the information on this poster your starting point and directional compass.

Organizational Basics

All companies start one of three ways regardless of formal organization chosen.

- **Solo:** This can take various forms such as freelance consultant, contractor, shop owner, tradesperson, broker, reseller, professional (e.g., accountant, lawyer, psychologist, physical therapist), etc. The key is that you will be responsible for all aspects of the business—from funding and budgeting to running daily operations.
- **Single Partner:** You and one other person go into business together and agree to split the work and investment (if needed) in some way. Funding, payment schedules, leadership

responsibilities, and daily involvement should be agreed upon in writing at the start.

- **Group:** There could be multiple people involved from the beginning with various investment level commitments, ownership stakes, management responsibilities, and daily functions. This environment can be high energy and supportive but tricky to set up and manage over time.

"There are different types of legal business structures you can choose for each category, so I've created a reference list that I'll pass around for everyone to take home," I explain. "Not only do you need to decide on an organizational designation, but the city, state and country in which to file. There are tax implications, legal considerations, filing costs, physical location requirements and other business operational issues to consider. Not all options on the list are available in every state.

"As a quick overview, sole proprietorships and partnerships are simple structures. They usually require the least number of filings and are the lowest cost to establish. Corporate structures typically require more paperwork, provide some legal protections and have more complex tax implications. Lastly, there are unique designations for specific types of businesses like non-profits, political organizations and co-ops.

Business Structure Options

- *Sole proprietorship*: You are the sole owner and not required to register as a separate business in most states (e.g., freelancers, attorneys, accountants, etc.).
- *Partnership*: Two or more people own a business and are categorized as general, limited liability or a family partnership (LP, LLP or FLP).
- *C corporation (C corp)*: A stand-alone legal entity owned by shareholders and that pays taxes. This reduces the risk for owners and investors while allowing the business to take on debt based on its financial strength.
- *S corporation (S corp)*: Similar to a C corp but profits and losses are passed through to shareholders.
- *Limited liability company (LLC)*: Owners are referred to as members and profits/losses are passed through on personal tax returns. This option also reduces risk for owners and investors.
- *L3C*: A subclass of LLC with a primary mission of charity while putting profits secondary. Establishing a business using this structure is only available in a handful of states. The IRS does not recognize this designation, but all fifty states do.
- *Charitable organization [501(c)(3)]*: A business must be organized as a corporation, association or trust, along with meeting certain criteria related to the management of profits and political participation.

- *Cooperative*: A group of equals that runs a business based on democratic principles. Not recognized by all states; various IRS rules apply to be considered under this classification.
- *Benefit corporation*: A fairly new corporate designation available in roughly half the states in the U.S. It provides legal protection for leadership to consider the interest of all stakeholders and not only shareholders. (More details are available at benefitcorp.net.)
- *Certified B corporation*: This is not an official IRS designation but rather a commitment by the organization to solve social and environmental problems certified by a third party called B Lab.
- *Political organization*: Typically designated as a 527 organization by the IRS, it's focused on influencing politics at any level.
- *Other tax-exempt organizations*: These include churches, farmer's cooperatives, tribal governments, HOAs, community sports teams, social clubs and similar groups. Refer to the IRS site at www.irs.gov for specifics.

"As a rule of thumb, it's easier to move from a basic structure to one that's more complex as opposed to the reverse. For example, Malik, if you start as a sole proprietor and decide to bring on an equal consulting partner, it's fairly simple to transition into an LLC or corporation.

"Once you legally establish the company, be sure to check state and local governmental agencies for registration requirements. They might include a city business license, industry license or professional license.

"You could also consult with industry governing bodies for required certifications such as pet breeding and training for you, Dylan, or health practitioner credentials and licenses as in your case, Kaya. Most likely, you can find professional organizations or business groups that can help you navigate the licensing landscape," I suggest.

"Some may have heard that the best place to incorporate is in Delaware because of the favorable tax code, simple filing requirements, and favorable legal environment.[11] However, many of these benefits don't help small startups out of the gate. You'll also probably have to register in your home state, so unless the benefits outweigh the drawbacks in your situation, it's probably wise to forego Delaware as an option. This is an important decision with tax and legal implications, so consult with a business attorney and accountant to understand all the options and filing requirements. There are a few other states with favorable incorporation environments like Wyoming, Nevada and South Dakota, so work with a professional to figure out your best option.

"Jade, you'll probably want to set up everything in the city and state where the food truck will physically operate most of the time since you'll need additional licenses for driving and food handling. Malik and Andres could consider states and countries that have favorable laws for their businesses since there will be limited geographical operational constraints. For Dylan and Kaya, if plans include taking on investors to help fund the business, incorporating in another state might be worth looking into. All of you should educate yourself on your options and how you might want to organize, and then consult with a business attorney and accountant to figure out the optimal solution and associated requirements.

"For the next step," I continue, "after deciding how you want to set up the stewardship of your new business, think about where you want to take it long term and an exit strategy. For example, Malik, if you want to start as an individual consultant but eventually plan to have a team of global consultants rivaling McKinsey and Company, then you'd make funding and business decisions that support big growth. If you want to keep it solo-focused on lifestyle and flexibility, then you'd move your business in that direction and budget accordingly. But if you choose the latter, be sure to have insurance and a backup plan if you can't work for an extended period due to physical issues, mental incapacitation, family demands, natural disasters or any number of unforeseen reasons."

"This brings us to the point of thinking about lifestyle and long-term objectives. *Are you creating a business so you have more control over your personal time with aspirations of the business basically running on its own? Do you see this as an opportunity to make significant money and increase your wealth? Is this meant to create a legacy that will be passed down for generations?* Whatever it is, be honest with yourself and your business partners, so you can agree on a common path and exit strategy.

"An exit strategy defines what happens to the business when you're done dealing with it. There is no right or wrong answer — only a destination. How you disembark the company's crazy train is your unique adventure to experience. However, it's extremely important to understand where and how you want to end the ride. Don't be like a Wild West outlaw, jumping off a moving train with a bag of loot and hoping for the best.

Jade chimes in, "I'm not sure how to use an exit strategy to make decisions about whether to buy or lease a food truck, or to hire employees. It's hard to see a connection."

"I absolutely get the disconnect, Jade," I respond. "As business owners, so many decisions are made every day with immediate or short-term implications; they don't seem to connect to an exit strategy. But small decisions build on one another to achieve bigger goals. For example, deciding on the quality of food, standardizing food prep processes and limiting the menu on a food truck can set you up for future expansion or franchising. On the other hand, if you want to experiment with new dishes, partner with other food providers or test out different locations in the county, those experiences can help you to open a brick-and-mortar restaurant in an ideal site. By keeping long-term objectives in the back of your mind, evaluating opportunities and make small strategic decisions along the way will keep you on track to achieve your exit goals.

"I've listed some common exit possibilities to consider on the whiteboard.

Exit Possibilities

- Offer ownership through a publicly traded market with an Initial Public Offering (IPO), or other financial market vehicles like a Special Purpose Acquisition Company (SPAC).
- Be acquired by another company for one or more valuable assets:
  - Protected defensible intellectual property
  - Market leadership
  - Customer list quantified by revenue, geography, size, market segment, etc.
  - Intellectual capital, which means the people in your ecosystem
  - Brand value
- Create a new parent company that supersedes the original business entity.
- Merge with or purchase another company or companies to create a new entity.
- Transfer ownership to employees through a financial plan like an Employee Stock Ownership Plan (ESOP).
- Transfer ownership to family or others in a closed private transaction.
- Close the business and sell the remaining assets.
- Sell the entire business, or sell it piecemeal to different buyers, on the open market.

"In some of these cases, the founders can negotiate roles in the new company or exit under an agreed-upon transition plan. In other cases, the founder might take on the role of CEO of a new corporation. No matter the outcome, your exit should be considered complete from your original startup business. Depending on the situation, it might serve you well to revisit the basics we just covered for the new entity.

"In summary, figure out your leadership and legal structure, long-term objective(s) and exit strategy. These will be the guiding lights providing direction when faced with strategic and difficult decisions. Once your company makes itself known to the world, market feedback and better opportunities might inspire a pivot that, in turn, changes the nature of your business. But you need a solid, focused starting point — including guardrails and end goals — that can light the path forward when things get muddled."

ASSIGNMENT 6
Structure and Exit Strategy

1. Identify the leadership organization and legal structure options you think will be the best fit for your business so we can work through some of the pros and cons. This will also help you have an informed discussion with the appropriate professionals when the time comes.
2. Outline the long-term strategic objective(s) for your business.
3. Contemplate your end game and formulate an exit strategy.

Chapter 7

Crystallize Your Vision

O ur next session addresses the last step of the strategic planning portion. I kick off the discussion with, "Your exercise was to determine organizational leadership and business structure, long-term goals and exit strategy. How did it go?"

"I thought it was going to take like fifteen minutes, but it took way longer," confesses **Dylan**.

Andres says, "I have so many different ideas, but I'm still not sure where I want this to go. Despite finishing the exercise, I'm sketchy about whether I can or even want to run a business. I'm worried that the first time things don't go right, I'll backslide into employee mode."

"Having doubts and second-guessing the startup path is fairly common, Andres," I reply. "It sounds like you're not quite sure you're ready to make the leap, but keep pushing through the process as if you were wholeheartedly committed, then decide how to move forward. You might watch kids playing with your toy and think this whole business idea is *totally lit!* What we're doing here is giving you a clearer picture of the opportunity and how to pursue it to better set you up for success.

"Putting yourself out there and taking a risk to start a new venture is scary. If you have a focus and vision of how the business will affect you and others, that will provide a strong sense of purpose and simplify daily decision-making.

"Another good question to ask is, *what community do you want your business to serve and be a part of?* A strong communal connection can provide support both personally and professionally. Okay, let's hear what everyone came up with. Again, there are no right or wrong answers."

Malik starts us off. "I'm already moving forward with a project deal I've been working on. That's a relief but looking past that point is difficult. I don't know if consulting is my passion and what I want to do forever, so I'm not sure where to go from here."

"The advice to 'follow your passion' is popular but doesn't work for everyone or in all situations," I comment. "Many people realize success *not* because they're passionate but because they *saw an opportunity, went after it and were rewarded for it.* That, in turn, created excitement for their business. Malik, it sounds like you're good at project management and can add value in that role. What is it you *don't* like? What's holding you back from turning it into a venture?"

"Well, I actually enjoy planning, executing and completing projects," replies Malik. "It's fun seeing something come together. I *don't* like begging and scratching for extremely limited resources in startups — whether it's mine or someone else's. And I *really* don't enjoy selling myself to companies."

"It seems like your sweet spot is working with growth or large companies," I affirm, "but you don't want to deal with the sales process, which is quite intimidating for most people. Does that get to the root of your problem? Or do you want to eventually do something else other than run a consulting business a year or two down the road?"

"I think it comes down to the sales and hustle side of owning my own business," admits Malik. "I don't mind working hard and putting in the hours on projects, but I don't like having to pitch my cred again and again. That's why I'm tired of working in startup companies. It's fun and exciting being a part of bringing innovative ideas to life, but the scrambling and instability are very stressful."

"Malik, the fact that you've actually worked in a startup environment is a big advantage when going it on your own," I say. "In fact, it's your key to success. Focus all that knowledge and experience on activities that energize and excite *you*. Outsourcing, automating and using nontraditional approaches to address things you don't like will help you stay motivated. For example, use your personal and professional network to find opportunities instead of driving sales through cold calling or submitting formal RFPs. You can also partner or contract with people that complement your skills, or become a subcontractor for a larger firm.

"Also, one benefit of running the show is you get to decide which customers to take on. It's always tempting to sign any contract when you're starting, just to have money coming in. But staying laser-focused on your ideal customer segment will make you happier and more successful in the long run. If you commit resources to a customer that's not a good fit, they won't be available when the right one comes along. We'll get into some tactics to help with sales and marketing, but for now, go ahead and share your leadership goals and exit strategies."

"I know right now I don't want to be a project manager until I retire," Malik says. "As we were talking, the idea of working as an employee again makes my body tense up. Building something of my own does energize me if I can push past my sales reluctance. You mentioned having a backup plan if something happened and I couldn't work. That made me rethink my long-term solopreneur strategy. So, I'm going to start out alone but not too far down the road, I want to bring on partners with the goal of staying small and private. In terms of my exit strategy, I want to sell the business at some point and do something else — like captain a yacht, help clean up the Great Pacific Garbage Patch or both."

"Okay, Malik, what I'm hearing from you is this: Your plan is to start as a solopreneur with the goal of partnering with others within two years and establishing an LLC or similar structure. The long-term vision is to be a thought leader in the tech industry and create an organization in which you work on big, innovative projects with a handpicked team of top-tier consultants. For an exit strategy, the end game is to keep the business private but grow it enough to sell the company or the assets to an outsider or offer a buyout to insiders. Is that explanation in the ballpark?"

"Yes, that really pulls it together for me," replies Malik. "I'm not sure about the industry leader part, but everything else sounds good."

"One good way to get out of having to constantly sell is by creating an authentic industry reputation so people seek you out," I explain. "There are, of course, other ways to position your business top of mind, so think creatively about other approaches. Selfishly, I want to get a ride on that yacht someday. Who's next?"

Kaya begins, "Okay, so Josh and I are going to be co-presidents of the company. We'll need some outside investment or a loan to buy equipment and software along with funding for marketing, so it's probably best if we incorporate. Long term, we both want to see our services available across the country. It would be great to turn this into a big successful enterprise that can reach underserved rural areas. I'm not sure at that point if we want to be running it day-to-day. Maybe we would sell to a company that can make it super successful."

"So excited for you two to get started, Kaya!" I exclaim. "As your business grows, you'll develop new skills and possibly find that either or both of you would like to continue managing the company so it stays true to the original mission. Also, consider exit strategies of going public or buying, selling to or merging with other companies. It's important to think through the pros and cons of each strategy and determine the best fit because these options require different financial strategies. It doesn't mean you can't shift in the future, given the right circumstances. But your end game affects how you should approach funding now and how to grow your business, especially when it comes to doling out ownership stakes. You might want to eventually create a non-profit arm that provides services to those with financial hardship," I suggest.

"Also, I want to circle back on the co-presidents idea. I understand you want an equal partnership, but it's important that you each take responsibility for an area of the business on a daily basis. Plus, you both need to set objectives that can be tracked and measured for accountability to each other and investors. Big decisions can be discussed and decided on together, but someone needs to have the final say and be responsible for execution.

"Your growth strategy will most likely involve multiple rounds of funding, so it's important to be stingy when distributing financial ownership of the business. By delineating areas of responsibility, it's easier to use Key Performance Indicators, or KPIs, and other tracking mechanisms to distribute small chunks of ownership at agreed-to time intervals. This helps ensure your commitment remains strong and doesn't reward those not contributing, which could create riffs within the leadership team. We'll talk more in-depth about financial management in the next meeting.

Dylan chimes in. "That totally fits with what I'm doing. I've been telling friends about our process, so two of my besties are in. We'll need some big money to get us going, so we have to figure out how this will work. I do know we need to be in posh areas in all the big cities around the country and even internationally. Our vision is to be Hilton of the doggy world, and our exit strategy is either selling to another company or going public."

"Fantastic, Dylan, I love that you're going big!" I declare. "Since you now have three founders and you're looking for outside cash infusion, it's important that you set up an organizational structure and goals for earning ownership in the company like Kaya's. You're probably looking at a C or S corporation as the best option out of the gate. Also, when starting out, you want to make important strategic decisions together while splitting up daily management responsibilities, but there might be a situation in which another founder is only the money person. Instead of committing time to managing the business, that person puts in agreed-to dollar amounts at certain intervals in exchange for an ownership stake.

"For example, one of you might be responsible for managing physical location logistics, which encompasses finding, setting up and managing properties. That person could take the title of chief operations officer. Another person would be responsible for creating the brand, promotional activities and dealing with customers as the chief marketing officer. The third might create processes, handle the financials and court investors with the title of chief executive officer.

"If you bring on an investor as part of the founding group, that person probably won't be involved in management at all or might act in an advisory capacity behind the scenes and as a board member. There are no rules about titles or organizational structure, but it's important to have descriptive monikers to convey who has decision-making authority to the outside world. Also, divide up the work so it plays to your strengths *and* all parties feel like they're adding value."

"Umm, would we all own one-third of the business at the beginning?" asks Dylan. "How do we know when everything kicks in? I mean, we need the investment money upfront, so does that investor own ninety percent of the company until years down the road? I'm not getting how this works."

"Whenever there's more than one person involved in founding a company, it's important to have a formal legal agreement that describes shares distribution, vesting, responsibilities and exits. The specifics and timing are up to those involved," I reply. "Be very stingy with ownership in your business so only small percentages are dispersed over time as the business grows. We'll be diving deeper into the details of handling financial management but know that it's critical to have an agreed-to structure in place should there be a falling-out down the road."

"That would never happen with us! No matter what, we'll always have each other's backs," declares Dylan.

"There's no doubt you feel that way now, and I hope that never changes," I say, "but things have gone sideways for more than one business that started with strong personal relationships. Plus, if you plan on getting funding from outside sources, you'll need to have a formal organizational structure in place. Don't worry, it's not as complex as it sounds, and don't take things personally."

Andres switches gears. "For me, it makes sense to start out on my own and see how things go. Maybe in the future, I'll want to partner with someone who can take my products to the people while I keep churning out new playthings, but I need to get a win first. My exit strategy is to sell off my inventions while keeping royalties coming in as long as my stuff keeps selling."

"Sounds like a solid plan to me, Andres," I remark. "When you're looking at options for taking products to market, be sure to analyze how much money you can make given best-case and worst-case scenarios. To start, you might want to use crowdfunding to sell your first invention. Once you learn more about how the industry works, it might make sense to license future toys to a big brand name or do it yourself by outsourcing the manufacturing and using a broker to distribute the toys. No matter how you go to market with your latest gadget, it's a good idea to have insurance and legal protections, so an S corp might be the best structure. Also, your timing of cash flows is important, so make sure everything aligns with your personal financial needs."

Jade pipes up. "I think I got this worked out. To start, I want to own the business by myself and hire people to work the truck with me based on how busy I think it will be. For an event, I might recruit my sister and brother-in-law, but for lunch in an office park, I can probably handle it by myself with a little prep work. Hopefully, I'll be busy and have to hire a staff. That would be a good problem to have! Ultimately my vision is to have a restaurant space that's a fun, fast casual kind of atmosphere. I'll probably keep the truck for special events and maybe catering. For my exit strategy, when I'm tired and ready to retire, I want to just sell everything. Even if my family is interested in taking it over, I want to sell it off and get out of the business."

"That's a great approach, Jade," I say. "I agree there's probably no need to bring on partners or investors at this stage, so consider an LLC when talking with an attorney about legal protections in the food industry. Let's talk a bit more about your long-term outlook. Do you only want to have the one location with the same type of food from your truck? You can choose from many options such as having several locations in a city, state or region. Another idea would be to franchise and create the next Panda Express or Chipotle. Or you could evolve into a regional restaurant ownership group, starting with the Asian barbecue place and expand into other restaurant concepts, so you have several diverse eateries in the portfolio. There is no right or wrong answer. The key is to be truthful with yourself about your aspirations."

"Those are good ideas," Jade responds, "but I keep thinking it's important for me to maintain control. If the business gets too big, then it might overwhelm me and stop being a fun outlet for my creative expression."

"Completely understandable," I say, "and you're not alone by any stretch. Almost all entrepreneurs struggle with balancing control and delegation, especially those who start out creating a consumable good by hand such as prepared food, handmade jewelry or clothing, or handcrafted furniture. What's the first step? To figure out *why you're bringing your creations into the world.* Next is to *plot a unique path to happiness and success on your terms.*

"No matter what path you choose, you need to maintain a balanced lifestyle as best as you can, which might mean entrusting others with your business. Transitioning from a producer to a leader can be highly challenging and involves overcoming a certain level of fear and sometimes fending off imposter syndrome — that is, feeling unprepared and undeserving of success. All entrepreneurs who begin working *in* the business to get it started and experience growth eventually reach a point of needing to shift their focus and work *on* the business to sustain long-term success.

"Maybe the direction for you, Jade, is to open a restaurant, grow your personal brand and then become an influencer, consultant or TV celebrity. You could write a series of cookbooks, add a line of business such as selling prepackaged meals or even be a traveling guest chef. I suggest listing the different directions you would be interested in taking the business. Think about how long you want to run it and commit to an exit plan. You never know what opportunities may come your way, like ex-cons Snoop Dogg and Martha Stewart doing a cooking show together. Who saw that coming? Still, you have to effectively convey what your interests are for others to help you along the way. No one does it alone."

"Wow! I didn't think about all those options," said Jade. "Definitely great ideas to consider, but I'm not sure I want to take on the pressure and stress of going big-time like Martha Stewart."

"I totally get it," I respond. "It's great that you recognize the responsibilities that come with a bigger operation. I was throwing out options so you'd consider possibilities that might be of interest. This decision isn't only about money but lifestyle, legacy, influence, family and anything else that's important to you. Remember, life isn't a dress rehearsal, so live it to the fullest. "Okay, enough Plato-level deep thinking. Let's move on to the next exercise."

Assignment Prep:
Finding Your Bottom Line

"When starting a business, everyone is excited, able to get along and full of optimism," I begin. "But as the days go by and challenges arise, disagreements are sure to follow. It's best to decide how you want to handle various types of situations upfront when everyone is feeling agreeable. Develop clear leadership guidelines so expectations, responsibilities, compensation, buyouts, incapacitation, inheritance and ownership specifics are understood by all involved. Having these in place will make the financial challenges and decisions that come with running a business easier to handle.

"This leads to our next step, addressing the financial planning for your startup. Consider what money and resources you'll need to get the business rolling and how much runway you have in your personal finances. It could be a small amount like what Malik is looking at, where funds come out of your savings or get charged to a credit card to cover licenses, a website, insurance, travel, phone and computer equipment, and contract management. Or you may need a substantial sum from outside investments or a loan to cover manufacturing, shipping, inventory, real estate and operational costs. That's the direction Kaya and Jade are headed.

"For our next meeting, be prepared to talk through your ideas for funding. Look at it from 10,000 feet — don't worry about estimating paperclips, printer ink or whiteboards. The important part is to develop a general budget that maps out *how much* money you'll need and *when* you'll need it. Follow that with how much money you expect to make over time through sales of your products or services. If there's a gap, come up with ideas on how to fill it."

ASSIGNMENT 7
Funding Plan

1. Estimate how much money you'll need to start and where it will come from. Work with a financial adviser or use software to understand cash flow and capture all expenditure categories.

   a. Figure out an initial two-year budget to get the business up and running.

   b. List your major expenses and estimate the costs. Don't forget to include potential line items such as founders' salaries, travel, legal and filing expenses, insurance, taxes and loan repayments or interest. This will give you an idea of *how much* money you'll need and *when*.

   c. Next, estimate what money will be coming in to cover these expenses — and make a profit — over those first two years.

2. If there are gaps in your budget, list potential ways to address them. Look at shifting the time frame or dollar amount of expenditures, increasing sales estimates, modifying the pricing strategy and/or securing additional funding.

   a. Outside investment will probably come from multiple sources, so make a list of options and target dollar range you hope to procure.

   b. Create a timeline for when new cash infusions will be needed and the estimated length of time to secure each of them, so you know when to start respective procurement cycles.

3. Try to finalize the structure of your business, such as S corporation or LLC, so you can better understand the financial options available and associated timing.

Chapter 8

Show Us the Funding

"Today we're going to explore funding options and how these decisions affect your business." I say to begin our next meeting. "Keep in mind, it might be necessary to pursue more than one financial strategy concurrently or over time. Of course, not all of these options will work or be available to everyone equally. It's highly unlikely that venture capitalists will write a $50 million check to first-time entrepreneurs just because you're a nice person with a snazzy presentation. Before we delve into your plans, let's walk through a few money ideas that have worked for others.

"The most common is **self-funding**, which involves getting out the hammer and breaking into your piggy bank. This option includes accessing savings, investments such as 401(k) plans (which have tax implications) or stocks, credit cards, personal loans and home equity loans. Be careful about how much personal money you invest. If your business doesn't start making money as planned, you'll need a financial safety net.

"**Business loans** come in many lengths, amounts and terms depending on your fiscal situation and collateral requirements. These can be small such as using a line of credit to help with cash flow issues and other short-term funding needs. Other situations might call for larger investments such as setting up physical space, buying equipment or purchasing raw materials, which might require assets to put up as collateral. Many flavors of loans are available including those based on future earnings of the business, convertible equity, assets and transactions. Remember, a startup is high risk, so expect interest rates to be much higher and loans harder to obtain than for an established business.

"One alternative to traditional bank loans is a **Peer to Peer or P2P loan**. This option can be used by an individual or under a business umbrella. It's funded by regular people using a third-party transaction platform versus a financial institution. According to Investopedia, the top sites for this are Peerform, Upstart, Prosper, Payoff and Funding Circle.[12] But be sure to do extensive research on which is best for your situation.

"Wait! You mean regular people compete with banks by putting up money to loan to businesses? Are they easier to get with more flexible payback terms?" Dylan asks.

"Yes, it gives regular people a chance to get in on the bottom floor of new ventures; it's not just available to wealthy people who pool their money," I reply. "Of course, there's risk that the money invested will be lost just like going to a casino, but hopefully odds are better by investing in someone's dream. The terms are specific to each platform and situation but usually more flexible than a traditional bank loan.

"Okay, the next option for those without much business experience who are just starting out is turning to **friends and family**. It involves securing money from people you know or are related to in the form of a loan or gift, or even in exchange for equity. Tread lightly and exchange money only with signed contracts in place. Your contracts must explain the risks and clearly state what the investor gets in return and when. Many relationships have been strained or ruined through personal business deals, so consider this option carefully.

"Believe it or not, there is such a thing as free money! It comes in the form of **gifts and grants** handed out mostly by institutions and governments. Purpose alignment is hard to find, but if what you're doing can advance an institution's mission, getting a gift or grant could be a great option. These can be accompanied by stipulations on how the funds will be used or may come with expectations of certain activities completed within a given time frame. This can be a lengthy process with specific deadlines, so do your research and plan well in advance.

"**Contests and prizes** are almost as good as a winning lottery ticket. Competitions come in all different shapes and sizes. Many contest sponsors want to extend their own research and development efforts by offering prize money for effective solutions to specific problems. They could also be interested in unearthing new investment or partnership opportunities. Of course, be sure to read the fine print before entering or accepting any winnings.

"**Customer prepayment** for goods or services can be a great option but is a delicate tool to wield. Basically, you pitch a customer for payment upfront on what will ultimately be delivered. For example, when promoting new books, popular authors will presell them several months in advance to help cover initial production run costs and give them an idea of how many to print. There is an element of trust on the customer's part, so beware if anything goes sideways; it can damage your ability to sell in the future. In the B-to-B world, it's likely your original design will need to be customized as a trade-off for the risk of buying an unproven product or service, but it's a great way to pay large expenses upfront."

"So, you're saying Dylan can presale her memberships like new gym locations do and I could presale my toy like a book," theorizes Andres.

"That's it exactly, Andres," I reply. "For your toy, another option is **crowdfunding**. It's a popular small business option that prepays makers for products and services. There is also the added bonus of a self-identifying test group with a proclivity to promote their 'finds' via word-of-mouth. Instead of exchanging ownership or rights in the company, you offer products or something of perceived value in exchange for a donation and the excitement of being one of the first to try something new. Over $34 billion worldwide, and counting, has been raised using these platforms.[13] The most popular ones are Kickstarter and Indiegogo, but many alternatives are available, including Patreon and Mightycause, which are for nonprofits.[14] Be sure to read the fine print since each has different terms such as the percentage charged in fees, deadlines for fundraising goals and minimum funding amounts.

"If you're in a business that requires a large initial capital investment such as heavy-duty machines, manufacturing equipment, a large-scale computer network and more, you might use **vendor financing** in the form of a loan or lease. This would be similar to a loan or lease from a car dealership.

"Another investment option approved by the federal government in 2016 for small businesses is **Regulation Crowdfunding or Regulation A.**[15] This is not available for companies prior to launching but could be obtained during the startup phase depending on financial viability. You'll find there are limits on the total amount raised within a twelve-month period, as well as restrictions on investors. Offerings can only be made through a single online platform that's registered with the SEC and FINRA[16] such as Wefunder, Start Engine or SeedInvest.

"**Incubators** generally provide guidance, networking opportunities, co-working space, resources and warm introductions for startups but usually don't have a set program to follow. Investment stakes are varied, and some don't take an ownership percentage at all, so do your research to ensure a good fit. Incubators can be a good alternative to going it alone, but you can't just walk in the door and expect to be greeted with open arms. Each has a unique acceptance process such as application reviews or top-secret invitations extended only to established companies.

"**Accelerators** are similar to incubators, but they usually take a small equity stake in exchange for acceptance in their concentrated development program. As the name implies, they take promising startups and put them through a condensed and intense process to realize significant growth over several months instead of years. Because few applicants are accepted into each class, there are enough dedicated resources to create high probabilities for success. Many accelerators are industry specific or offer focused tracks of interest to their investors. Global Accelerator Network is a good resource to get you started.

"How do you decide between an accelerator versus an incubator for your business?" asks Jade.

"It depends on what you're looking for from a support standpoint and based on your company vision," I explain. "If you want to go big time with investors and potentially take the company public, then an accelerator would be a good path. On the other hand, if you want guidance, insights and access to people that could help you grow without pressure of meeting an aggressive revenue objective, then an incubator would be a better fit. Also, there are a couple more options.

"**Angel investors** are generally individuals or a loosely organized group of people who want to support the entrepreneurial dream by investing funds in small startups. The level of investor involvement in a business can range from completely hands-off to daily operational decision-making. Terms are typically negotiated on a case-by-case basis with a variety of loan and equity options available. This is often the first step to additional venture capital investment, or VC money as it's commonly referred to, down the road. Beware, though. Once you commit to the VC world, you and your leadership team answer to investors, which makes it almost impossible to extract the company from those long-term financial commitments and move in a different direction.

"If you're ready to play the big time and deliver on prescribed deadlines, then accepting money from professional investors is an option. **Venture Capitalists** pool money from individuals and organizations with the understanding that they will seek out, analyze and invest in opportunities before the public has access to them. Companies usually must show high growth rates supported by viable business models to get this level of funding — unless the founders are well-connected. Investment typically comes in a series of rounds over time. As the dollar amounts increase, so do expectations of the return on investment and the more ownership stake you have to give away in the form of dilution. Once VCs get involved, they usually look for a five to seven-year time frame for a payout. That happens either by the business going public through an IPO or SPAC, or it's purchased by a company with deep pockets such as Procter & Gamble, Yum! Brands, Microsoft, Alphabet (Google) or Meta (Facebook).

Funding Options Summary

- Self-Funding
- Business Loans
- Peer to Peer Loans
- Friends and Family
- Gifts and Grants
- Contests and Prizes
- Customer Pre-Payment
- Crowdfunding
- Vendor Financing
- Regulation Crowdfunding (or Regulation A)
- Incubators
- Accelerators
- Angel Investors
- Venture Capitalists

"No matter the type of funding, it's essential that you watch your cash flow carefully. Never think of investments as Vegas winnings to be splurged. The failed startup trail of tears is littered with companies that got significant cash infusions, only to spend it on extravagant office space, over-the-top expenses and too many employees. I can't stress enough the importance of becoming self-sustaining as quickly as possible. That means your revenues cover your monthly expenses, including any loan payments and founder payouts that is, your salary.

"All right, enough lecturing, let's see what ideas each of you came up with. Tell us which structure will be best suited for your business and share your initial funding ideas. If you want feedback on how any of these investment ideas might work for you, throw them out for the group to discuss."

Says **Jade** excitedly, "That was a lot of info to take in at once. I had no idea there were so many options. Now I'm excited about how quickly I can get my business up and running. Maybe I can get vendor financing for my truck and some of the equipment. How great would that be! Anyway, I'm going with an LLC structure for insurance purposes and to protect myself from lawsuits. To get the business *rolling*, pun intended, I thought I'd use savings and personal credit cards, but now I'm going to explore other options."

"That all sounds great, Jade," I say. "Regarding a food truck, you might look for a used one that's for sale by owner and ask if you can pay through a private financing agreement. The titleholder would sell you the truck, but instead of writing a big check, you would make installment payments over time — just like a bank loan. Also, look into government and bank auctions to see if any are up for bid but be sure to examine the truck's condition before buying it. There may also be affordable leasing opportunities. Get creative about other truck options like sharing ownership with a breakfast or dessert food company or exploring rent-to-purchase."

"I'll jump in next," says **Malik**, "since my costs are low and my financing plan is simple. Between savings and credit cards, I should have no problem covering my startup costs. Also, I'm going to negotiate a portion of the contract be paid upfront and additional payments made at monthly intervals. At this point, I don't envision renting office space or having other major cash outlays, so I feel comfortable not securing outside funding support."

"Seems like a well-thought-out and responsible approach, Malik," I respond. "Going forward, though, watch your cash run rate. In this case, it's the amount of money you'll need to cover expenses over a defined period. You'll probably have big chunks of expenses for items such as travel, insurance and estimated taxes. You might get to the point where you're using subcontractors that need to be paid quickly. What if a client's payments don't arrive in time to cover everything? You need backup ideas.

"Also, a deal might come along that's impossible to pass up but only pays when the contract is completed. Your invoice then has to make it through the client payment process, which can be anywhere from an additional fifteen to one hundred and eighty days after receipt. That means for a six-month contract, you should figure an estimated run rate of ten months to cover all your business expenses. Also, when negotiating contracts, don't be afraid to propose options such as partial payment after specific deliverables, bonuses for achieving certain goals and immediate reimbursement for expenses such as travel. Now, what's your business structure?"

"I didn't consider payment details like that, so definitely something to think about when negotiating contracts," answers Malik. "Anyway, I plan on setting up as an LLC, so I can get the proper business insurance required of contractors by most larger companies. Also, it's a simple enough structure that allows me to easily bring on future partners if I decide to go in that direction."

"Cool, Malik, I'll go next," says **Dylan**. "First off, for our doggy spa company, we plan to set up an S corporation so we can formalize our organization like you suggested. We'll definitely need outside funding, so this just makes sense. To finance our bougie biz, we thought we'd try to get a loan along with funds from friends and family. But after going through those options you mentioned, we might look at crowdfunding."

"Keep in mind, Dylan, that you can pursue multiple funding options simultaneously," I remind her. "P2P might be a good avenue to explore. Also, angel investors might be interested in this opportunity and would give you access to someone with business experience. When looking for investors, focus on people with similar areas of business expertise, like luxury accommodations, resort activities, spa amenities or pet services. Real estate investors might make good partners if they can provide the physical locations for a percentage of revenues.

"Also, ensure you have a personality match. When you meet with angels, you need to be interviewing them as much as they are analyzing you. Crowdfunding is worth a look, and presales could work for you, too. Providing discounted rates with prepurchase service packages or memberships is an option. Don't rule out grants and contests, either. Think about partnerships with boutique hotels or health retreats as well. A final note, with all these potential players you should consider forming as a C corp initially. It will cost a bit more but should be easier in the long run to handle all the funding and management complexities. Work with legal and financial professionals to figure out the best option."

"All that sounds awesome, but here's a question," says Dylan. "How do you find angels?"

"For those not in Silicon Valley, it can seem like you're searching for Sasquatch," I respond. "However, the timing is great after the pandemic worldwide shutdown. Angel investors have been forced to find opportunities virtually instead of through local in-person meetings and networking activities. AngelList is a place to start. You can also explore Pipeline Angels and Tech Coast Angels.[17] Another good way to find these elusive, early-stage investors is to network locally at industry and startup events. You can find those via online searches and on Meetup.com. Once you get further along, it might be worth exploring incubators and accelerators. Most importantly, don't get discouraged if you're getting a lot of no's before finding the right partner. Don't be afraid to ask for feedback, but know the triggers VCs are looking for can vary significantly from one to the next. Decline an investment offer if the terms are one-sided, ethics don't align or personalities don't mesh."

Andres jumps in next. "I want to keep my toy business simple, so I'll start out as a sole proprietorship. Initially, I was thinking of selling my idea on Etsy or through a co-op, but now you have me rethinking things."

"I'm excited to hear that, Andres," I respond. "Crowdfunding could be a great option. It allows you to figure out if people are interested in your toy while getting money up front to cover manufacturing and shipping costs. As a bonus, this will help you find a prime ultra-targeted audience to become your evangelists. Be sure to keep supporters in the loop if there are delays to promised deadlines. Once you successfully deliver by under-promising and over-delivering, you'll have an opportunity to make changes to the original toy based on their feedback. Then you can do another round of preorder crowdfunding to test the next iteration. This is a good way to manage costs, do testing and build your brand early on before you must invest heavily in manufacturing, distribution and marketing.

"Another route is licensing. You build the prototype and gather market data including usability, engagement levels, target market, price range and so on. Once you have a proof of concept, it can be pitched to toy, gaming or app companies. Be sure to work with a patent attorney to file protections with the U.S. Patent and Trademark Office first.[18] It's important to cover licensing issues in discussions and contracts like the percentage of gross profits you get paid, timing of payments, time to market, penalties for non-compliance, marketing commitments, distribution, availability, code fixes and version management. A business attorney is good to have on your side through these types of negotiations."

"We might be able to do some of those things with our in-home technology, too," notes **Kaya**. "For structure, our plan is to incorporate, but we're not sure if a C or S corp is best. For funding, it will be a mashup of things. Josh thinks we can get discounted used equipment, and it sounds like vendor financing might be an option too. Initially, we were thinking that personal and bank loans could get us started, but maybe getting a P2P loan would be better."

"I suggest you work with a business attorney and accountant to understand the best corporate designation and location for you since they have different filing requirements and tax implications," I say. "Also, the medical field has unique regulations by state so find professionals with experience in the industry. Regarding funding, P2P would be a good avenue to pursue. Equity crowdfunding is also worth investigating.

"Once your services are rolled out, you might consider various customer payment options. For example, you might offer a discount to people if they pay six or twelve months in advance. If you charge $3,000 per month for Package A in-home care, you could offer a six-month prepayment of $16,000. If you go this route, be sure to cover termination clauses, refund policies, changes to the level of care and other possible contract variables. It helps to have an attorney draw up standard contracts and set up protection against possible lawsuits. You'll want a good insurance policy too in case of accidents, malfunctions, human error, etc. Also, make sure you ramp up quickly enough to hit breakeven and cover your costs before running out of that upfront cash." I take a deep breath, knowing we accomplished a lot in this session.

"That was a lot of information to analyze and tough decisions to think through. I'd recommend setting a funding strategy to start and then work on making it pay off versus chasing random leads that well-meaning friends throw out at a barbecue. More than one founder has been frustrated and burned out by constantly creating and delivering pitch decks instead of growing their business.

"As if I haven't said it enough, I highly recommend all of you work with an accountant and business attorney who specialize in startup businesses. Preferably, they have expertise in your industry but it's not a deal breaker. Make sure they align with your level of risk-taking. Interpreting this country's expansive tax code and laws isn't black and white; they exist in a grey area. Some professionals lean toward strict interpretation of regulations and laws while others see more creative opportunities, with each approach carrying positive/negative consequences. Ask questions and keep interviewing until you're in alignment with people that share similar risk profiles.

"A couple of examples are Uber and Napster. Uber disregarded the established laws and regulations governing taxis and vehicles for hire, boldly arguing that because they offered a marketplace via a smartphone app, taxi licensing restrictions didn't apply to their service. As you probably know, they have successfully expanded rideshare services around the globe facing limited interference from legal institutions with a few places like Austin, Denmark, Hungary and Bulgaria as notable exceptions. The taxi and shuttle ecosystem had to adjust and has lost millions while Uber and other rideshare apps have exploded in size and valuation.

"On the flip side, Napster didn't fare so well. It provided free software that allowed users to download copyright-protected music for free and without the permission of the recording studios or artists. Napster claimed protection under 'fair-use' doctrine, which allows certain uses of copyrighted materials without permission, since it only facilitated the transaction. Due to massive sales losses, Napster was eventually sued by A&M Records and lost its argument in court.[19] Soon after, Napster shut down and filed for bankruptcy, despite the brand name living on. These examples show how upstart companies challenged established laws and the status quo, but with very different outcomes.

"What a great discussion. Let's all stand up, shake the arms and legs, jump up and down, and do some neck rolls. We need to clear our heads and get the blood flowing as we move on to more creative pursuits," I conclude.

Assignment Prep: Name That Biz

"It's time to create your company image," I say excitedly. "This image includes branding, messaging and graphics. Before you can file all the necessary paperwork and make the new business official, it needs a name and identity. Don't think of it only as a nickname with a cute tattoo; it's a branding strategy that will dictate how the world perceives your business. Are you a Walmart or Macy's? A Taco Bell or Morton's? A Nike or Vans?

"The first step is deciding what to call your company. It might make sense in one scenario to have a single brand name for the business and everything you sell. In another, it could be effective to have a company name that runs in the background while building brand recognition around individual products/services. For instance, General Electric offers a wide range of consumer and business products using one umbrella company brand. Proctor & Gamble, on the other hand, is the company name with many products offered up as individual brands such as Charmin, Duracell, Crest, Pampers and Tide.

This distinction is important because it directs your marketing and sales strategy. If in doubt, go with one name. Later, you can always create a corporate identity like Facebook did with Meta and Google did with Alphabet.

"After you decide on the nomenclature, start brainstorming company names along with those for your product or service if applicable. For any name, the general guide rails are to keep it short, easy to remember, relatable in definition with a pleasing cadence. Let the creative juices flow! It doesn't need to be an actual known word but one you make up, such as Google, TiVo, Kleenex or Pepsi. In fact, those are actually easier to trademark. Or you could create a longer name but use an acronym to make it easier to say, type into a browser and remember. IBM started as International Business Machines[20] and ESPN was condensed from Entertainment and Sports Programming Network.[21] Once you have a list of ten to twenty possibilities, it's time to do some branding research."

I begin outlining brainstorming actions. "Your next step is to complete internet searches for other companies using the names on your list. If they're in a similar business, cross off that name and move on. If it's in a different industry and you really like the name, then keep it on your list for now.

"Next, once you narrow down the list of names, check a domain provider such as NameStation, Easy DNS or GoDaddy to see if the URLs for the names you chose are available. The .com extension is preferable but if taken, look for other top-level domains, or TLDs, such as .net, .biz, .inc, .llc, .pub, .services, .studio, .restaurant and so on. No matter your business type and offer, it's essential to have a website presence; this way, you'll own and control the domain name for your brand so someone else doesn't. If you can't find a suitable URL, mark that name off your list and move on.

"Then take your pared-down list and check the U.S. Patent and Trademark Office database at USPTO.gov to ensure your preferred name isn't already legally claimed. Businesses can have similar names if they're trademarked in different industry categories, so you might still be able to use it. Most businesses have an internet presence these days, but a few still operate 'old-school style,' so it's a good idea to check.

"Lastly, check your list against local city and/or county licensing offices and against secretary of state filings where the business will be registered and headquartered. You want to ensure a name isn't already in use. If you find a registered name that's similar but not exact, there's nothing keeping you from moving forward with it; however, it should probably drop down on your list.

"At this point in the process, you should be down to one or only a handful of suitable business names. If several are still on the table, then consider which best represents what you'll be selling, how easy it is to spell and remember and how long it is, knowing that shorter is better. Try it out with trusted friends, family and networks to get their reactions. Asking others is a good way to get different perspectives and find out if it's offensive in any way. Still, be wary of who you share it with. You don't want someone purchasing the domain name from under you, pointing it to a one-page website full of paid links or setting up fake social media accounts.

"The reason for all these steps this early in your business is to avoid confusion in the market, lawsuits and big costs associated with a name change in the future. Running a business is tough enough without creating additional headaches down the road.

"At our next session, please share your chosen name but come with a couple of backup ideas in case issues arise that you might have missed."

ASSIGNMENT 8
In Search of a Name

1. Brainstorm company names along with those for your product or service, if applicable.

2. Do internet searches for other companies using the names on your list.

3. Check a domain provider such as NameStation, Easy DNS, Hover or GoDaddy to see if the URLs for the names you chose are available. You can get creative with TLDs other than the traditional .com, .net or .org.

4. Take your pared-down list and check the U.S. Patent and Trademark Office database to ensure your preferred name isn't already legally claimed.

5. Check your list against local and state filings where the business will be registered.

Branding is More Than a Logo

After everyone has arrived for our meeting, I walk in adorned with a University of Colorado baseball hat, San Diego Padres sandal-shaped earrings, U.S. Open PGA Torrey Pines golf shirt with a Nike swoosh on the sleeve, Levi 501 jeans and Brooks Ghost running shoes. "Does anyone notice anything about what I'm wearing?"

"Love the Padres earrings. Where did you get them?" asks **Kaya**.

"Thanks!" I reply. "Found them at a little store that used to be next to the stadium. Sadly, it's not there anymore."

Andres pipes up. "Being a Cal guy, I did notice the Buffs hat."

"Sending out that old Pac-12 Conference love back at ya, Andres," I smile, tipping my hat.

Jade chimes in, too. "Do you like the Brooks Ghost running shoes? I've been looking for new ones, and a couple of people recommended them."

"Yes!" I say, "They're my new favorite running shoe line. I use newer ones on the road and an older pair when hitting the sand. Anyone else have thoughts?"

Dylan eagerly responds by asking, "Are those retro 501s? I just found a pair at my fav recycled fashion store, the Buffalo Exchange, and love them!"

"Yep, but I found *these* in the back of my *closet*," I quip with a wry smile. "I wore these items to show how important branding is to any entity. It's not just a logo; it's the *feeling* people get when interacting with your company. For example, when you saw the Padres earrings, Kaya, I could see your energy level go up. It probably reminded you of the camaraderie of cheering on a team and spending time with friends or family. You recalled the excitement of being at the ballpark as well as the sense of community there, right?"

Kaya responds, "I never really thought about it like that, but, yes, going to the Padres games represents all those things to me."

"And Andres," I say, looking at him. "You felt a sense of pride and belonging that evoked a fist-pumping competitive fire for UC Berkeley when you saw my Buffs hat, right?"

"Hundred percent, but it's all chill," replies Andres. "I'm not going to arm-wrestle you unless you want to!"

Everyone laughed at the thought of a short, not-so-young woman taking on a six-foot, 210-pound, thirtysomething surfer.

"That's the kind of passion and visceral reaction to strive for with your business," I emphasize. "You want people to gush about how their lives have been positively affected by buying what you're selling. The branding journey starts with a name, so what did everyone come up with?"

Jade speaks up first. "I narrowed it down to three names and want to get input from the group before making a final decision. The idea of *quisine* came to mind replacing the "c" with a "q" like in the variant barbeque but the domain was taken. So, I played around with different naming ideas settling on two iterations and one unique idea. The first one is Quasine Kitchen with quasine.kitchen as the URL, the second is Quasina using quasina.com and the last is AQ Fuse with aqfuse.com domain name that hints at a fusion restaurant. What do you all think?"

"Quasina is fresh! Reminds me of exotic home cooking if that's a thing," remarks Dylan.

Kaya jumps in. "AQ Fuse is easy to remember and sounds like it would have a cool vibe with interesting flavors."

Andres pipes up, "I could totally see me and the boys going to the Fuse for post-surfing sustenance."

"They all sound interesting to me," says Malik, "but if I had to choose, it's AQ Fuse. It piques my curiosity. Quasina is a close second for the same reasons but with an international flair."

"Seems like it's between AQ Fuse and Quasina," I conclude. "Looking at it from a marketing perspective, you could do many fun things with both names. AQ Fuse seems a little easier to remember and should be simple enough to spell in a search engine. It rolls off the tongue and would be a good choice if you went with it, Jade."

Malik eagerly goes next. "I'd like input as well but not sure if I want to use my last name or go with something made up. My gut tells me to go with Ramile Engineering or Consulting since my name carries a little equity in the industry. I also settled on Proneer, which is made-up like Twinkie, Sony, Tervis or Kodak, followed by either Solutions or Professionals. The domains proneer.solutions and proneerpro.com are available. If I go with my own name and want to bring people on board in the future, will I need to change the name like law firms do? Don't think I like the of idea Ramile, Smith, Jones, Garcia and Associates."

"That's certainly a valid concern, Malik," I reply. "Many large professional organizations hang out the partner title like a carrot offering a stake in ownership and name on the door. They become incentives to produce and bring in new business. The downside to that, besides the expense and hassle of name changes, is if a partner makes a big mistake or breaks the law, it could damage the entire firm's reputation. Read up on Arthur Andersen to get an idea of how things can turn ugly.[22] If you go with a new random name, it will take time to build brand awareness, but think of it as a long-term investment. Two very different options to mull over.

"Before we move on, let's take a quick vote on Malik's names. How many like Ramile Consulting or Engineering?" Two hands go up. "Who prefers Proneer Solutions or Professionals?" Two hands are raised. "Without a clear winner, I'll weigh in as a vote for Proneer Solutions. It gives you more flexibility as your business grows, Malik, and presents your company as a 'problem solver' versus a 'professional' in a field like dentistry or law. Typically, when companies contract for project management, they want recommendations and execution on plans to accomplish specific activities, not just to get expert advice."

Dylan speaks up next. "Okay, I really like Pawmazing for a name but don't know if the owner of the URL Pawmazing.com will sell. I could go with Pawmazing.Club or another dot-something, but it might be confusing. We also came up with Furbulous Paws, but the dot-com version isn't available at all. Many of the names we came up with were already taken, so we thought adding 'club' to either name would make it chicer anyway. So, it's between Furbulous Paws Club and Furmazing Club, both using dot-club instead of dot-com."

I respond first. "If you're excited about a name, but it's already in use, one option is to explore different spellings. But that can get confusing, as you pointed out. The last thing you want is people getting frustrated trying to find your business online. I like the club idea as a way to convey exclusivity and high-end personalized service."

Dylan replies, "The club idea came to me when doing my research. When I typed in a URL that wasn't available, a list of other ideas came up and dot-club was one I liked. Can you believe there are over five hundred domain extensions available?! Anyway, I did an online trademark search, and nothing came up for either name, so I'm rolling with these. Which would the group choose?"

Jade spoke up. "The first thing I thought of when you mentioned Furmazing Club was an infomercial and someone shouting, 'It's Furmazing! It slices, dices, peels and chops!' But you could twist that into a fun slogan and logo."

"Yeah, it could definitely become an earworm thing if you drop some beats on it," Andres suggests, making techno hip-hop sounds.

"Furbulous Paws sounds more sophisticated to me," comments Kaya. "It brings to mind pet pedicures, spa days, infused water, and exotic salon coat colors and cuts."

Malik adds, "I don't have a strong feeling toward one over the other, but if I had to pick, I'd go with the Paws Club option. Can actually see Ariana Grande calling out Furbulous Paws on Insta."

"Some good feedback so far, Dylan," I say. "I suggest you talk with your two business partners and settle on a name everyone can get behind. This is a good opportunity to figure out how you'll discuss difficult issues and make decisions once the business is running full throttle and things are moving at lightning speed. It's imperative that there is clear communication among all of you, and that everyone is respectfully heard."

"So, I got stuck," admits **Andres**. "After whittling down to four names, my brain got tired of thinking about it, so I worked on my toy. The names that made the cut are The Brain Outfitters with dot-com, LBOLabs.com, Left Brain Box ending in dot-com, or BrainPlay.Toys. Of course, some of the names I really liked were already taken because 'brain' and 'play' are popular search words."

"Coming up with a good name is harder than it seems," I say. "The diversity of the names around your main theme of 'brain' is impressive. Quick question, did you include 'the' in

Brain Outfitters because someone is already using BrainOutfitters.com?"

"Yes, but I liked it, so I kept it on the list," replies Andres." I know it could be confusing and potentially a legal issue. Having said it out loud it sounds like a really bad idea, so I'll scratch that one as an option. But what does everyone think of the other three choices?"

"Is BrainPlay.com taken as well?" asks Malik.

"No, it was a premium domain and crazy expensive!" exclaims Andres. "There are no registered trademarks on the four options, according to the USPTO site."

"Okay, then Brain Play Toys gets my vote; it's fun to say and easy to remember," adds Malik. "Wait a minute, do you think you'll invent other things that aren't toys like 3-D tools or add-ons to smart home technology? If so, I think LBO Labs is a better fit."

"Yeah, some of my other ideas aren't really toys, so I guess I should leave it open to work on other projects," says Andres.

"You could consider Brain Play Toys as a product line and one of your other options as the company name, Andres," I suggest. "That way, you don't have to give up a moniker you really like, and it provides flexibility to roll out products that aren't toys. It's a fairly common approach in the consumer goods space. If you choose that route, then buy both domain names. Use your product line name as the focus of marketing, promotion and sales, and then use the company name mainly for legal and banking purposes. It seems like extra work at the beginning, but if you roll out other product lines, it actually becomes easier," I explain.

"Hmmm, that has potential," replies Andres. "I could use Brain Play Toys for my first few toy ideas and LBO Labs as the company name,"

"It definitely makes sense. Maybe you'll be a Hasbro or Mattel one day!" exclaims Kaya.

"That would be so amazing to be a Mattel, Andres! Definitely go for it," chimes in Dylan.

"I like that approach, too, Andres," affirms **Kaya**. "And I'm last to go. For our business we plan on using only a company name. Josh and I had many naming discussions and finally settled on capturing the idea of intelligent home care. We came up with four options to run by the group. They are Intelligent Home Care using dot-com, IntelHomeHealth.com, MySmart.Healthcare, and IHCPros.com."

"Typing long names into search and having to think about spelling on a phone is a hassle, so that first option is not working for me," comments Jade. "I like IHC Pros, but it could be any business, including plumbers or carpet cleaners. For the other two, I could go either way but are kind of long, too."

"I think I get your business; you go in and help people understand how to live healthier, right?" asks Dylan.

"Basically, yes," answers Kaya. "Using the latest technology, we'll help people improve nutrition, create workouts and mental health spaces, and ensure their living environment isn't toxic. Also, we can provide support for those dealing with health issues and recovering from surgery."

"Okay, then Intel Home Health gets my vote," replies Dylan.

"I second that," chimes in Jade.

"Well, being a tech guy, My Smart Health Care makes me think of rigging up a house with automated or advanced intelligent technology. It seems more along the lines of what you plan to do," offers Malik.

Jade comments, "I like that one, too. Either works for me."

Andres says, "Yeah, I'm not sure, but I like the two with *health* in the name. IHC Pros could be anything and Intelligent Home Care is long and cumbersome like Dylan said."

"Okay, Kaya, that's good input to take back to Josh and make a decision," I say. "Like Dylan, this will be a good first test of your partnership and how best to work together. I'd drop Intel Home Health from the list since there's a global technology company called Intel that could demand you cease and desist with the name. If you want to better understand the risks before discarding it completely, discuss the pros and cons with a business attorney.

"You all did a great job! Deciding on a name requires creativity and diligence, but making a good choice is worth it in the end. Trust me, you don't want to go through the hassle of a name change once you've established the brand and have a solid customer base. It would require time, resources and money that could be used to continue growing your business. And you definitely don't want to deal with a lawsuit.

"Before making a final decision, run through the different ways each name can impact your business. This can help you focus on the best option," I suggest. Then I bring out a list of questions to ponder. "You don't have to check off each one of these. Rather, I offer points to consider when making your final decision.

Naming Considerations

- How do you want people to think and feel when engaging with and talking about your business? For example, trustworthy and competent; warm and caring; cutting edge and cool; knowledgeable and intelligent; sophisticated and elite.
- Is the name easy to remember?
- Does the name easily connect to the essence of your business?
- Is the name easy to spell, type, and speak so it supports accurate keyboard or voice entry?
- Does the name translate well into Spanish? (Chevrolet's Nova meant No Go in Spanish) The U.S. has the second-largest number of Spanish speakers in the world, so they might make up a significant part of your customer base.*
- Will it be the name of your company, your product, or both?

---

*Sonia Thompson, "The U.S. Has The Second-Largest Population Of Spanish Speakers—How To Equip Your Brand To Serve Them," Forbes, May 27, 2021, https://www.forbes.com/sites/soniathompson/2021/05/27/the-us-has-the-second-largest-population-of-spanish-speakers-how-to-equip-your-brand-to-serve-them

"Take time between now and the next session to finalize your names," I instruct. "If there are any name changes since your initial research, then run through the infringement checklist again of local, state and federal registrations to ensure it's not already in use. If it's all clear, then go ahead and purchase domain names and submit the federal, state and local required legal/regulatory documentation for your business.

"If your finances are in order, go ahead and apply for a business Employee Identification Number, or EIN, with the IRS[23] which you'll need to open a business checking account under the newly minted name. Going forward, use the business account to pay for expenses and deposit any incoming money. Start exploring other payment processing solutions you might need like Venmo, PayPal or Square. If you purchase items for the company with your personal money, keep the receipts for your records, make note of what was purchased and pay yourself back via the business account. This will make it easier and cleaner to track all business revenues and expenditures while keeping personal finances separate. Plus, you'll need to submit quarterly estimated tax payments to the appropriate government authorities using an EIN number or your social security number, depending on how you set up your business."

Dylan asks, "If we plan on getting funding from friends, family, investors and loans but don't have any of it yet, how do we get all these things set up?"

"Good question, Dylan," I respond. "What you'll need to do is have the partners use personal accounts to pay for necessary expenses up front until funds can be secured. Once you get outside money and establish financial accounts, the business can pay you back and any ongoing subscriptions can be transferred over. For example, if you purchase a few domain names from Go Daddy with your personal credit card, be sure to login and change the contact, account information and payment information once your business is funded. Also, get reimbursed unless you agree to different investment terms upfront. If you don't get paid back for business expenditures you can probably deduct them on your taxes. Strategize with an accountant for the best course of action."

"While we're on the subject of domains, after purchasing a URL you can initially leave it parked with the domain registrar. Eventually, however, it will need to point somewhere like a website, social media page, blog or 'Coming Soon' web page. It's important to secure the domain name(s) you want as soon as possible to prevent any pirating of your brand. Whatever name you decide, evaluate whether to buy variations. For example, AT&T has att.com as the main site but also owns atandt.com, which points to the same home page. Also consider common misspellings and typos such as gogle.com or amazon.com that a nefarious person might use to misrepresent your business," I explain.

<h2 style="text-align:center">Assignment Prep:
Creating a Brand and Identity</h2>

"The last step in our journey is to create a brand image that visually conveys the distinctive vision and USP of your business, so go back and read those again. The design elements of your brand will be used in website creation, social media accounts, and other marketing and promotional activities. The ultimate goal is to create a standard that captures your company's essence so the brand becomes easily recognizable. It would include a graphic design guide complete with logo (including black-and-white and reversed-out versions), font type, company colors, sizing, mark usage, tagline usage and so on.

"For our final session, we'll focus on logo design and the basics of your brand guidebook. Development of the marketing strategy details will be quick and easy for some, while others will need a more extensive plan, which will be part of your next phase activities after our last meeting.

"The easiest way to begin creating a logo graphic is to throw out ideas, then narrow them down using a functional checklist. Use this handout with key pointers to guide your design thinking."

Logo Creation Guide

Colors: Pick colors that complement each other and conjure feelings consistent with your brand message. For example, blue infers trustworthiness while green implies nature. Color Wheel Pro[24] has a good general guide to explain the psychology of colors and will match those that visually work well together.

Shape: Try to keep the graphic design in the broad shape of a circle or square as opposed to being wide or tall. It's easier to work within a variety of layouts (e.g., website, advertising, promotional items). This isn't a deal breaker, so don't discard odd-shaped designs that are impactful.

Variations: Look at the design both in color and black-and-white to ensure design characteristics aren't lost if printed in books, newspapers, pamphlets or other monochromatic mediums. If you farm out the design task, be sure to ask for both versions.

Sizing: Shrink and enlarge the logo design to see if it's still recognizable and doesn't distort as the size changes. Find a screen bigger than a computer monitor, such as a projection screen or large TV, when viewing the expanded version. Also, shrink it down to the size of a favicon (the webpage icon on your browser tabs) to see if it's recognizable. If not, is a portion of the logo recognizable? That portion could be cropped for small images like the colorful *G* used by Google. But if it looks like a jumbled mess, move on to another option.

Tagline: If you want to include a tagline with the logo (e.g., Nike swoosh with *Just Do It*, KFC with *It's Finger Lickin' Good*), create one version with verbiage and another without for a variety of uses. You'll need an icon-only version in various marketing situations and where the logo size is significantly reduced. Also, if you want to change the tagline in the future without modifying the graphics, it becomes a simple edit.

Marks: If you create a unique logo and own the rights to it, be sure to include a trademark [TM] or service mark [SM] on the graphic. It doesn't need to be registered with the United States Patent and Trademark Office (USPTO) for basic common law protection since it becomes automatic once it's used, but if you want statutory protection (i.e., at the federal level) you'll need to file with the government. If you decide to officially register to gain statutory protection for your mark and get approval, then use the registered trademark symbol [®] to identify it. It's a good idea to use TM or SM until approval is granted. When using marks you're asserting a claim of ownership. That holds true *unless* it infringes on another mark, so double-check on the USPTO site at www.uspto.gov to see if a similar design has been registered. There, you can also find details on how to use the different marks. A business attorney or registration service can help out if you have questions or concerns.

"Plenty of options are available to develop a logo design. You can work directly with freelancers, third-party logo creation sites or do it yourself. Once you're happy with the logo, make sure to get the original files which are either in vector or raster format.[25] Also ask for the HTML/RGB color designations for computers and CMYK for print, so you can maintain consistency across all design efforts.

"Lastly, ensure you'll own the rights before any work begins. When money is exchanged, use a third-party agreement or signed contract that addresses costs, number of revisions, ownership and basic legalese. Having a startup attorney in your court comes in handy in this case.

"Now, to prepare for our final meeting, let's work on brand imaging — the logo, color, and font — and don't be shy to ask for input from people. Feel free to narrow your selection to a few options, and discuss them with the group next time we meet."

ASSIGNMENT 9
Company Image Creation

1. Finalize the naming convention.
2. Develop brand imaging for your company and/or products.
    a) Create the logo.
    b) Decide on the color scheme.
    c) Pick a font or fonts to use in the logo.
    d) Decide if you'll use a tagline, then create logo images with and without it.
    e) Decide on marks to use.

Chapter 10

Shout Out to the World

I t's our last official meeting!" I declare. "Can you believe it? The time has flown by, and all of you have been so engaged and enthusiastic. It seems like just a few days ago we were at the beginning of our journey at Startup Week.

"It's been an exciting adventure so let's get started on the last piece of the puzzle. To refresh everyone's memory, the assignment was to finalize business names and then create logos, including colors and fonts, for use in your marketing and promotional materials. I hope you had fun developing a brand image that tells the world about your company. The visuals should also evoke feelings for your brand that align with your vision and USP.

"Let's go around the group and see what you came up with. Share the names you've chosen, restate your vision and show us your logo ideas."

"I'll go first since mine's fairly simple," says **Kaya**. "We brainstormed some more and settled on My Smart Care for a name using the .care extension. Our vision is to help individuals live healthier and use technology to improve nutrition, lifestyle and the home environment. People still might wonder exactly what we do, but this logo felt right. What do you think? Does it fit?"

I respond first. "Before we get into a discussion, I want to throw out an idea. Many times, companies use a tagline to help further define what they do and provide a theme for marketing, planning and execution. It might be good to establish what your company can do for people with the addition of a descriptive tagline.

"Remember the Nike swoosh I mentioned in the last meeting? In 1988 it was a niche brand and was losing market share to Reebok. After the addition of *Just Do It* and a national marketing campaign Nike took off and increased sales 1,000% over the next ten years.[26] When people would see the icon alone, those words automatically popped into their heads and vice versa. In your case, Kaya, the logo could be the circle graphic with the company name and a tagline underneath, or put together in another creative combination. Some tagline ideas to get you started are 'Intelligent Lifestyle,' 'Customized Health Care' or 'Technology for a Healthy Home.' Anyone else have thoughts they would like to share?"

"I like the circle design, so if you use only the graphic it's still unique to your company," comments Jade. Also, if you add a tagline like 'Intelligent Lifestyle' it should be smaller and probably a different color than the company name so people can differentiate the two."

Andres agrees. "That absolutely works. The logo doesn't scream health care or healthy lifestyle, it's just a cool design. Adding a tagline would definitely help to clarify what your company does."

Dylan chimes in. "It looks professional but I'm wondering if it will be too busy with the business name and tagline at the bottom. You might want to try putting the name in an arch on top and the tagline underneath."

"I agree with everyone that a tagline would be helpful," says **Malik**. "I'll go next and share my ideas. I went back and forth on Ramile Consulting and Proneer Solutions, so I figured your input could help me make a final decision. I don't see bringing on a partner right away, if ever, so I'm leaning toward Ramile Consulting. Of course, if I do decide to partner with someone, we won't have to wrangle with the whole partner naming issue if I use Proneer. Here are logo concepts for both names. Thoughts?"

"Okay, before we discuss and take a vote, remind us of what your vision is," I ask Malik.

"Sure," he replies. "I want to be a catalyst for business transformation by understanding client challenges and desired outcomes to create and deliver customized solutions. The idea is for the graphic to convey how we propel the client forward. So, who likes the Proneer name over RC?" Three hands go up. "Okay, how many prefer the Proneer logo with all the angles?" One hand goes up. "What about the circle version? Two hands are raised. "So, I guess the rest of you like both or neither."

"For what it's worth, I like Ramile Consulting because it's clean and simple." says Andres. "I don't really have a preference with the Proneer logos."

"That's a tough decision," says Kaya. "I'm leaning toward Proneer with the circle. It's unique and I like the little person-looking thing. If you go with Ramile, I prefer the one with the arrow. Up and away like a superhero!"

"Same; I agree with Kaya," states Jade.

Dylan is last to comment. "I think Proneer works the best with either logo version. If I had to pick one, the circle is probably my fav."

"Some general comments come to mind," I say. "Your idea of adding a secondary line for Proneer Solutions is helpful because it clarifies what the business is all about. Also, I like the dot in the Proneer angles version because it pushes people to the URL and reinforces the identity. If you go with the Ramile Consulting version in the circle, I'd recommend finding another font for the name because it's difficult to read. Lastly, *Solutions* seems more proactive than *Consulting* but I think either will work for you."

"I'll go next," says **Dylan**. "We all got together and had a real convo about who wanted to be a part of this adventure, and three of us are all in. Others may join later or help with raising money, so this was a perfect time to weed out those that aren't serious. Anyway, we decided on Furbulous Paws Club with furbopaws.com as our link. As far as the logo goes, we couldn't agree on graphics or colors, so we decided to let the group weigh in."

"These are very creative!" I exclaim. "Before I give you my feedback, let's take a vote. How many like the one with the puffy cloud background?" Two hands go up. "Okay, how many for the crown?" Three hands go up. "And how many for the running dog?" Two hands go up. "Hmmm, by my count some voted more than once. Hey, I get it, all three of these are good. They convey sophistication and exclusivity. Dylan, remind us of your company vision?"

"Sure," she replies. "It's to create pampering and nurturing experiences for humans and their pets. We're going to be THE bougie pet spa in town."

"It seems they all hit the mark in conveying your vision, so let's dig into the designs," I say. "When the designs are shrunk to smartphone app icon size, I think the crown and dog icons could be used and are easily recognizable. Shrink them down to be sure. As with Malik's version, make sure the script fonts are easy to read, so test them with a few friends and family. The only other point that might help you decide is that the dog icon could imply that your spas will be for canines only, so the other two might provide more long-term flexibility.

"When you take this feedback to your partners, decide if you can pick one version everyone agrees on. If not, figure out a way to determine a winner. Some options are using an online research service, an in-person polling company, or have your team talk with friends and family with pets. Generally, it's hard for a group to agree on a design, so great job! Oh, and would suggest getting the URL for Furbulous Paws Club spelled out and point it to furbopaws.com to protect your brand. Furbo is great for marketing but you want to make sure a competitor or squatter doesn't get the long version."

Jade jumps in. "I'll go next. I decided on the name AQ Fuse, thanks to your input. There were several different logo ideas that I liked but was able to narrow it down to just two.

"After all the discussion today and looking at them again, I'm feeling one more than the other, but I'd still like your input. Can I get a show of hands for the traditional pagoda Asian look?" Two hands go up. "How about the second triangle abstract version?" Two hands go up.

"Which one did you like the best, Jade?" asks Kaya.

"Initially, I was all in on the pagoda look, but after checking out other Asian and barbecue restaurant logos and seeing the creative work all of you have done, I think the triangle would better *sear* into people's memory," quips Jade. "The idea behind it is that my flavors are unique so my logo should convey fresh, hipster fusion food instead of a traditional Asian restaurant."

"The artsy look fits better with your vision of creating healthy comfort food with a twist, Kaya," I agree. "It's simple, easily recognizable and unique. The design is clean and not too busy, so it should shrink down or blow up in size without distortions. Plus, I think it gives you some flexibility with colors and shading to develop a memorable brand. Don't forget to note the RGB, CMYK and HTML designations for all your colors and the font names. The same goes for everyone."

Andres closes it out. "I decided to go with LBO Labs for the company name using the domain of LBO-Labs.com and BrainPlay.Games for the product line. I had a friend help me with design ideas and I like them all, so I want input from the group to help me narrow it down."

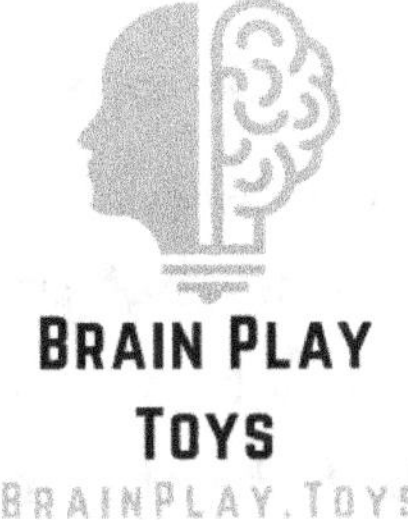

I respond by saying, "The naming convention sounds like a great idea, Andres. It gives you freedom to market any number of your ideas without diluting the brand or creating confusion in your customers' minds. What feedback does the group have?"

Comments Malik, "For the Labs version I like the lightbulb because it's simple and says innovation to me. Since it seems like your toys are STEAM-related and in keeping with the lightbulb theme, I think the little robot works best for Brain Play."

Dylan jumps in. "I think the lightbulb for LBO Labs is sleek and inspiring, but all three options are cool. When people see the Gucci "GG," they instantly know it's a Gucci purse. Hasbro has that same deal with toys. I think you could do something similar and pull it off with the little robot bulb guy."

"Oh, yeah, that's a good point, Dylan," inserts Jade. "Do you want your logo to be on the toys and recognizable like Beanie Baby or on the packaging like Lego? If it's on the toy, then I think the lightbulb robot version works best. If it's on the packaging, then any of them could work, but I'm leaning toward the bubble gum brain,"

Malik adds, "I'm with the group so far with the LBO Labs preferences. For Brain Play, my preference is the bubble gum brain, too, because it's so unusual."

"I think I'm the only one that prefers the Labs logo that looks like jacks, but the swirly lightbulb works, too," says Kaya. "For the toy logo I think it should line up with the company Labs version you choose, so the robot should go with the lightbulb and gumballs with the jacks."

"Great feedback from everyone," I say. "Kaya made a great suggestion to look at how the two play together. It's not imperative that there's a connection, but if you're having trouble choosing, that's one way to narrow down the choices. Again, don't forget to capture your color and font specifics so the design can be easily shared with web designers, graphic artists, partners, vendors and more. Be sure that you all add applicable trademark notations to your final logo and name designs.

"Now you're ready to finish up all the online setup and turn everything you've learned into action," I conclude. "Next steps depend on the type of business and how far along you are in launching it. Since Malik has a contract opportunity lined up, he only needs to address a few things to get rolling. He has to finalize contract management details, obtain needed insurance, file new business documents and set up a payment process.

"Jade, on the other hand, will have several project tracks going at once such as legal and licensing; obtaining a truck and funding; setting up the menu, cooking practices and transaction processing; and creating a marketing launch plan. Dylan and Kaya will also have multiple streams of activities leading up to launch. And Andres, you'll be setting up the legal and insurance side followed by testing and funding efforts. These will ultimately lead to launching or selling your product.

"I've very much enjoyed our time together and watching your ideas come to life. Go launch your enterprises knowing you have a leg up on most first-time entrepreneurs. Keep in mind, everyone makes mistakes running a business, but it's how you respond to those mistakes that make the difference.

"I can't wait to see what you all accomplish in the future. Before we go, I'll wrap everything up for you in a summary checklist that will keep you on track."

Chapter 11

Launch Checklist

I leave the group with these final thoughts: "We've worked through a lot together and I've thrown a ton of information at you in a short time, so it may be hard to remember everything. Just like packing for an extended trip, it's good to have a checklist when launching a new business.

"On this poster are some important points that could apply to your startup. Some of these actions will need to be done *before* making the first sale while others can be handled on a rolling basis depending on your unique business situation. I'll provide a quick synopsis of each to help determine which apply to your startup."

Final Checklist

World According to Uncle Sam

- ☐ Establish the Business
- ☐ Collect Taxes
- ☐ Pay Taxes
- ☐ Understand Tax Implications
- ☐ ID Sneaky Government Requirements

Navigating the Legal System

- ☐ Protecting Intellectual Property
- ☐ Generate Contracts & Common Docs
- ☐ Know Customer Protection Laws

Planning for Profit

- ☐ Obtain Insurance Coverage
- ☐ Calculate Cash Flow and Budget
- ☐ Manage Transactions

Make the Right Connections

- ☐ Bring Together the Right People
- ☐ Set up Communications Solutions

"The section **World According to Uncle Sam** highlights things government entities might require of your business. There are many different payments, deadlines and filings to figure out. The details depend on the type of structure and city where your company is established and operates. Software programs, accountants and outsourcing firms can help you set up everything. You'll want to dig deeper in these important areas because it's always better to pay upfront rather than risk big penalties down the road.

"The first thing everyone should do is formally **Establish the Business.** To do this, secure an EIN from the IRS. File and pay for any required licenses at the federal, state and local levels. Even if you start out as a sole proprietor or contractor like Malik, you'll probably need to file a basic registration. Also, investigate programs and designations intended to help traditionally disadvantaged groups, such as women-owned, minority-owned and veteran-owned businesses. Understand the requirements and begin the validation process as soon as possible because it can take a year or more to get certified.

"Another thing everyone needs to do is figure how to **Collect Taxes.** Understand the tax rates, when they apply, and when payments are due for each of the products and services you offer. Determine if you want to cover any of these, like sales tax, in the pricing to your customer similar to inclusive price tags found at farmer's markets. Or, you can add them on during the payment process as a separate line-item cost like what you see at restaurants and retail stores.

"Once collected you need to **Pay Taxes** to the right entities at the right time. There are different types at the federal, state and local levels. Like an Easter egg hunt, you need to seek and find all those that apply to your business. Some business taxes are based on actual earnings while others are estimated, so be sure you know what's required and when. Those 'eggs' are easier to spot when it comes to personal taxes. The challenge is not finding them but paying them — in this case, submitting withholding estimates due throughout each tax year. Be aware that annual IRS federal tax filings for businesses are typically March 15 instead of the April 15 deadline for personal taxes.

"Research or find a good accountant to **Understand Tax Implications** on your business and personal finances. The IRS and other taxing entities categorize people as self-employed, stockholders, LLPs or LLCs, independent contractors, employees, etc., each carrying unique tax implications. For example, Jade, if you set up an LLC, profits can flow through the business and to the partners, who would pay taxes at their individual rates. On the other hand, an S corporation would pay taxes on the profits while listing payments to employees such as salary, executive bonuses or other form of compensation as an expense. Kaya and Dylan you need to understand how cash will flow and its implications before legally setting up your company.

"There can be a multitude of local and state taxes and fees you never knew existed, so dig up those **Sneaky Government Requirements**. Examples include Social Security, workers' compensation, inspection fees, certifications and hazardous waste disposal fees. If you work with contractors, partners, vendors or other third parties, be sure to track all financial transactions and submit required filings annually with the IRS and other government entities. For example, in 2021 you would've had to file and send 1099 forms to contractors you paid more than $600 to by the end of January. Dylan, you'll have many different layers to all your transactions as you build your fur baby spa, so it would be especially wise to get professional help.

"The next section highlights important things to think about while **Navigating the Legal System**. As any good Tik Tok parrot would do, I again highly recommend hiring a local business attorney that can provide guidance.

"If you created something unique for the business explore **Protecting Intellectual Property** using patents, copyrights and trademarks. Not every idea can be protected, so find out more at the U.S. Patent and Trademark Office and U.S. Copyright Office websites. Andres, it's important for you to hire an experienced attorney who can research and write an ironclad patent to protect against patent trolls extorting money from you in the future. It typically takes several years to get a patent approved and must be defended in court, so be sure the time and effort are appropriate for your business.

"Generate Contracts and Common Documents that might be used regularly in your business (e.g., nondisclosure agreements, vendor contracts, work agreements, contractor agreements, warranties, return policies). This will save you time and legal fees in the long run.

"Make sure you **Know Customer Protection Laws** applicable to your business both as a buyer and seller. Be sure to check federal, state and local levels related to sales, warranties and guarantees that you need to abide by in your line of business. Examples are state lemon laws for cars and gift card expiration laws by state and at the federal level.

"At its core, running a successful business comes down to turning a profit. That means bringing in more money than goes out, in other words **Planning for Profit**.

"Protect yourself, your business and your assets by **Obtaining Insurance Coverage**. Various types protect the physical environment and others cover services and leadership. In some cases, your business might be required to carry certain types and amounts of coverage before a customer will sign a contract, as we talked about for you Malik. Also, be sure to address health and disability coverage for yourself and any employees.

"Unless your business is cash sales only there will be lag time between the purchase and when you receive payment. It's common for businesses to spend money before selling anything with any number of different payment options available. To keep your startup afloat it's very important to **Calculate Cash Flow and Budget**. Most businesses, especially large corporations, have lengthy internal payment processes so it can be anywhere from 15 to 180 days before receiving payments. Make sure you calculate that into your cash flow models, especially if you have vendor or subcontractor costs to cover before getting paid. Malik, Kaya and Andres, you need to be keenly aware of these factors and bake them into your pricing and processes.

"It's imperative that you effectively **Manage Transactions** by monitoring cash flow. Ensure all business and personal finances are separate. Keep receipts for all transactions and note the details (e.g., date, purpose, attendees, associated customer account, location) to easily track and itemize expenses. Also, set up financial accounts such as credit card, debit card, payment processing and payroll account. Figure out how the business will process incoming and outgoing transactions, and make sure to account for those costs in your pricing and budget. Jade, this is a big decision to make before you open. Will you be cashless, cash-only or a hybrid? Which credit cards will you accept since they charge different transaction percentages and fees? Will your bank charge a fee for giving you dollars and coins for a cash drawer? When calculating your prices, don't forget transaction processing fees from providers like Square and PayPal.

"Effective communications both internally and externally are very important to success as is nurturing a supportive network, so **Make the Right Connections**.

"Consider personal attributes when partnering, hiring company leaders, recruiting early members of the team, and working with contractors. **Bringing Together the Right People** is so important to success; it's one of the critical factors that VCs consider when investing[27] and has been cited as one of the main reasons for business failure.[28] Qualities to look for when establishing significant professional relationships (compiled from numerous sources and entrepreneurial reflections) include:

- Agreeable personalities
- Similar work ethic
- Respect for each other's differing opinions
- Trustworthiness
- Similar personal and business code

- Complementary skills and experiences
- Appreciation for what others bring to the table
- Shared vision for the business
- Similar or complementary risk tolerance profiles

"**Establish Communications Solutions** for your business separately from your personal life as best you can. Items to consider only for business use are phone number(s), emails using your domain name (not gmail.com or yahoo.com), a P.O. box, a fax number (yes, some industries still require them), a customer support service and an answering service.

"I can't stress enough the importance of bringing together a solid team of experts that includes legal counsel, accounting professionals, insurance brokers, mentors and industry experts. It's always better to pay a little upfront than a lot more down the road. Most of all, make sure you take care of your mental and physical health to help make your startup journey a huge success.

"A peer support system is enormously beneficial for entrepreneurs, so you might consider staying in touch with everyone in this group. Friends and family want to be supportive, but they can't easily relate to what you're going through. Each of you understands the others' businesses and goals, so continuing to help each other roll out your startups would be invaluable.

"Good luck to all of you. *You got this!* It's going to be an amazing adventure."

Epilogue

Where Are They Now?

After the success and enthusiasm around our original Beyond Startup Week team, I decided to continue encouraging other would-be entrepreneurs to take the big leap by adding group meetings to the process. You can find information at www.Navabiz.com.

In the meantime, let's check in with our original five; this is how things have progressed in the six months since we met.

Andres put the finishing touches on the first of his STEAM

Brain Play Games product and took his MVP model to the kids. They played with it, broke it, shared it and provided meaningful feedback to create the version Andres is taking to market. To build his first toy, he worked with a small firm that specializes in creating crowdfunding profiles, and Andres sold out the first release. Due to supply chain delays his company, LBO Labs, hasn't delivered the toy yet. However, Andres has kept his supporters informed and made good on all the other promises in his funding profile. I have my t-shirt and look forward to getting the toy soon!

Dylan and her besties agreed to an equity earning plan that includes goals, activities and KPIs. They each have responsibility for specific areas of the business with one founder contributing startup funds and drumming up interest from several angel investors. The team has been busy pitching the concept of partnering with targeted lodging and spa chains while exploring the idea of accrediting boutique hotels and B & Bs as certified Furbulous

Paws Club members. They're considering hiring an executive director to help evaluate properties and accelerate the launch time. Members of the original Beyond Startup Week group will be invited to the grand opening that Dylan plans to hold within the year.

Kaya and Josh will license current technologies to get their business started, and several of those companies have agreed to favorable leasing options for the necessary equipment. My Smart Care has been working with insurance companies, Medicare and Medicaid to determine what is covered and what expenses are out of pocket. That's no easy feat. Additionally, the team is awaiting responses on several grants and special low-interest loans. They've contracted with several in-home

Personalized Healthy Home Care™

professionals to test their program and provide input for improvement. My Smart Care plans to soft-launch in a couple of months and, if all goes well, begin the rollout of a big metro push three to six months later.

Malik finished his first trial project as an individual contractor, which led to an extended nine-month opportunity. He was talking with a friend and colleague about Proneer Solutions, and she expressed interest in possibly pooling resources to go after bigger contract opportunities together. They agreed to feel out the market for their combined skill set and talk again in six months

about joining forces. Because of that, Malik decided to move forward with the name Proneer Solutions with buy-in from his potential partner. They created a basic website for clients with a lead management plan. It also gives potential contractors or partners an idea of what they do since some colleagues from previous jobs have been looking for contractors or new opportunities themselves.

Jade decided to go the food truck route. AQ Fuse has become a popular stop at several office parks around the city. Jade found a truck owner who was getting out of the business and scored a good deal. She got funding through a P2P funding site and found a willing family member to help work the truck. They've made contacts in the business parks that have led to catering several private events. These provide a good profit margin because customers are charged upfront by headcount, leading to fewer prep hours per plate and less food waste.

Jade is a little surprised that she enjoys interacting with customers every day and gets the added bonus of hearing their feedback and ideas firsthand. She's going to try out new dishes that only require a couple of additional base ingredients, so if they don't catch on her profits don't take a hit. It took time to figure out the best processes to serve people quickly and is still a work in progress, but going cashless made that part much easier. Jade is thinking about participating in a couple of big events, like the county fair and balloon festival, to see if they're worth the time and investment. As a side note, Jade's pineapple barbecue lettuce boat is the best!

Definitions are based on how these entries were used in the context of this book. If you are looking for generic or expanded explanations refer to dictionaries, reference materials or online resources.

A

Accelerators: Intense and concentrated startup development programs focused on fast-tracking promising businesses usually in exchange for an investment stake.

Ads: Common marketing abbreviation for "advertisements" like you hear on the radio or see on TV and social media.

Affiliates: Businesses that promote products, services or other companies in exchange for some type of compensation.

Aggregator: A business or service that gathers information or things and presents/delivers them to potential consumers or customers.

Agile: A type of project management process that uses short iterative efforts (sprints). Teams create pieces of a larger project, launch, gather feedback, re-evaluate then start the process again.

B

B-to-B (also B2B): An abbreviation for business-to-business interactions or transactions.

Barrier to Entry: A superior way to meet a need or want in the marketplace that is difficult for would-be competitors to replicate.

Best Practices: Established standards that have been determined to optimize output.

Boards: A group of advisers that helps guide businesses in various capacities. All public companies are required to have a Board of Directors but there are other versions suitable for different organizations.[29]

Bougie: Extravagant and associated with upper middle class.

Brick-and-Mortar: Permanent physical space in which a business operates, usually a commercial building of some sort. The phrase harkens back to the days when small individual shops were built with bricks and held together with mortar.

Business Components: Functional areas of an organization or piece parts that contribute to the final product or service.

C

Cherry Pick: Select only those things of interest or relevance.

Competitive Landscape: The combination of businesses that offer the same or similar products or services and those providing substitutes targeting the same group of potential customers.

Consumer Sector: The group in a marketplace identified as individuals versus businesses or governments.

Contractors: Individuals hired to do specified work for a limited time under agreed to terms and are not classified as employees under current laws and regulations.

Co-op: A cooperative which is a business entity comprised of a group benefiting from working together as a whole.

Co-opetition: When competitors decide to work together usually on a product, service, project or event.

Coworking Space: Buildings that have been arranged to create shareable meeting and work areas that individuals or businesses can rent out hourly, daily, monthly or longer.

Customer Pool: Potential, current and former customers of a business.

D

Dead Link: URL address that when clicked on comes up as a site not found, an error page, or takes you to a domain provider that is parking it - purchased by a customer that hasn't pointed it to a working website.

Deeper Dive: Doing more research or gathering more data on an issue, product or project.

Defensible Product or Service: A business offering that is difficult for others to duplicate. It can be in the form of a patent, unique process, exclusive collaboration or contract, rare ingredient, or something else that is challenging to replicate.

Direct Competitor(s): Another business offering similar products or services competing for the same discretionary customer dollars.

Distributor: An entity that typically gathers products, organizes, warehouses and delivers them directly to customer locations or other outlets where they are eventually sold to the end customer.

E

Early Adopters: People that like to be the first to try and buy new products or services, typically in a specific category like tech gadgets.

Employee Identification Number (EIN): The U.S. government identifier for businesses similar to social security numbers for individuals.

Evangelists: People that are big fans and supporters of your company, products and/or services who proactively espouse perceived benefits and positive experiences.

Exit Strategy: The way founders or leaders plan to close or transition the original business.

F

Facilitating: Leading or moderating meetings, groups or sessions.

Franchising: Expanding a business by replicating it in other geographic locations or virtual spaces. These can be owned and operated by the original company, franchisee investors or a combination of both.

Freelancing: Someone that provides services to individuals or companies for a specific period of time or project on a contractual basis.

Functional Area: Formal or informal groups in a business that can be identified by what activities they perform. For example, marketing, customer service, sales or tech support.

G

Gross Profit: Net sales (revenues less returns and damaged goods) minus the cost of making, delivering and selling products or services. It can be calculated differently using various inputs for analysis at the company, division, product, geographic area or sales team levels.

H

H-1B Visa: A federal program that allows companies to hire nonimmigrant workers for special occupation needs.

I

Impostor Syndrome: When those in leadership or expert positions feel like they aren't qualified for their role, thus undeserving of success, and will eventually be exposed as a fraud.

Incubator: An organization that provides resources and support for startups selected through a vetting process.

Independent Contractor: Individuals that agree to work with a company on a contractual basis instead of as an employee.

Indirect Competitor(s): Another business offering different products or services competing for the same discretionary customer dollars. For example, a sit-down Italian family restaurant is an indirect competitor of a fast-casual Mexican place a few blocks away.

Inflection Points: Important decisions or actions in the timeline of a business that impacts its trajectory.

Instructional Track: A group of educational sessions available over a specified period that carry some type of theme or common base throughout.

K

Key Performance Indicators (KPIs): Standard or unique tracking mechanisms used to measure goals and activities that are important to employee, company and partner success.

L

Legal Business Structure: Formal organizational designation recognized by various levels of government.

Life Cycle Stage: A point in the timeline of a business, product or product line that is characterized by a particular level of growth and development.

M

Marketplace: A place where prospects, customers and businesses come together to exchange things for value.

Minimum Viable Product (MVP): The point at which a new product is developed enough to deliver the essential functions so it can be released and works for end users.

N

Newbie Founder (also Newbie Entrepreneur): Someone starting a business from scratch for the first time.

Niche: A portion of the market where a product or service meets the specific needs or wants of an identifiable group.

Non-Compliance: Not executing and delivering as agreed to in a contract, or not complying as directed by laws and regulations.

Non-Dilutive Capital: Money provided to a company that doesn't require ownership stake in exchange.

O

Operations: The behind-the-scenes activities in a business that deliver products or services to customers.

Outcompete: When one product or service meets the needs and desires of customers in the market better than all the others that tried to do the same.

Outsourcing: When a company hires an external person or entity to take on a project or activity on a contractual basis.

Ownership Stake: The percentage or shares of a company that a person or business investor owns.

P

Peer to Peer Loans (P2P): Loans comprised of multiple investors pooling money to fund individual companies using a third-party platform.

Pitch Deck: Typically, a group of PowerPoint slides created for a presentation to potential business investors.

Pivot: When a product, service or business significantly changes what it delivers to customers and shifts market position.

Pop-up: An easily assembled temporary storefront used to sell goods or services indoors or outdoors.

Proof of Concept: It's the manifestation of an idea brought to the point where people can see and interact with a product or service without it being fully completed.

Prototype: The point in the development of a new product where a working design can be used to test the usability and functionality.

S

STEAM: An educational approach that incorporates the arts into the original STEM model, which includes science, technology, engineering and mathematics.

Subcontractor: An individual or entity that works with a main contractor under an agreement to deliver goods or services to a business.

T

Tax Implications: Actions and decisions made in the course of operating a business that can increase or decrease a company's tax obligations.

Time to Market: The period from concept or licensing agreement until the product or service is launched and made available for consumption.

Top-Level Domains (TLD): The extension or ending after the "dot" of a main URL for a website such as ".com".

U

Unique Selling Proposition (USP): A statement describing what a business offers that is different from competitors.

Usability: The level of difficulty or applicability users experience when engaged with a product or service.

User Interface (UI): The presentation software that people interact with to use underlying technology solutions.

V

Valuation: An amount the investor community thinks a privately held company is worth or will be worth in the future. The types of things they consider are: defensible products or services, competitive landscape, assets, customer base, leadership team, intellectual capital and projected future revenues.

Venture: A new business entity.

Venture Capital: Collective monies invested in high-risk private small to medium sized companies with the expectation of significant growth and ultimately delivering significant financial returns.

Venture Capitalists (VCs): Private equity investors that research companies for high growth potential and provide financial support in exchange for equity.

Version Management: Determining what features and functionality will be in each version of a product or service. It also includes timing of releases, updates and support.

Vision Statement: Succinct description of what a business aspires to be.

W

Widget: Common business term used to describe a generic product.

Index

[1] Robert Fairlie and Sameeksha Desai, "2019 Early-Stage Entrepreneurship in the United States," Kauffman Indicators of Entrepreneurship, Ewing Marion Kauffman Foundation: Kansas City, June 2020.

[2] "The Top 12 Reasons Startups Fail," CB Insights, August 3, 2021, https://www.cbinsights.com/research/startup-failure-reasons-top/.

[3] "Search Engine Market Share United States of America," Statcounter, December 2021, https://gs.statcounter.com/search-engine-market-share.

[4] Additional resources for small businesses can be found at SCORE: https://www.score.org and U.S. Small Business Administration (SBA): https://www.sba.gov.

[5] Minda Zetlin, "Oprah Winfrey Says You Should Ask Yourself This 1 Question Before You Do Absolutely Anything," *Inc. Magazine*, April 8, 2019, https://www.inc.com/minda-zetlin/oprah-winfrey-asks-herself-this-question-before-starting-anything.html.

[6] "Herb & Rolling: The Birth of Southwest Airlines," Southwest Airlines 50 Years, https://southwest50.com/our-stories/when-herb-met-rollin-the-birth-of-southwest-airlines/.

[7] "Purpose, Vision, and The Southwest Way," Southwest Airlines, January 26, 2022, https://www.southwestairlinesinvestorrelations.com/our-company/purpose-vision-and-the-southwest-way. (Verified by Melanie Graham, email to author, August 15, 2022.)

[8] Sandeep Babu, "Startup Statistics 2023 - The Numbers You Need to Know," Small Business Trends, December 27, 2022, https://smallbiztrends.com/2022/12/startup-statistics.html.

9 Meredith Wood, "Raising Capital for Startups: 8 Statistics That Will Surprise You," Fundera, February 3, 2020, https://www.fundera.com/resources/startup-funding-statistics.

10 Anita Campbell, "69 Percent of U.S. Entrepreneurs Start Their Businesses at Home," Small Business Trends, Jan 20, 2020.

11 "Delaware Corporate Law," Delaware.gov, https://corplaw.delaware.gov.

12 Allison Bethel, "Best Peer-to-Peer Lending," Investopedia, October 6, 2021, https://www.investopedia.com/articles/investing/092315/7-best-peertopeer-lending-websites.asp.

13 Mary Kearl, "Best Crowdfunding Platforms," Investopedia, June 10, 2021, https://www.investopedia.com/best-crowdfunding-platforms-5079933.

14 Ibid.

15 "Regulation A," U.S. Securities and Exchange Commission, April 28, 2022, https://www.sec.gov/smallbusiness/exemptofferings/rega.

16 "Regulation Crowdfunding: A Small Entity Compliance Guide for Issuers," U.S. Securities and Exchange Commission, April 15, 2017, https://www.sec.gov/info/smallbus/secg/rccomplianceguide-051316.htm

17 Angel funding resources: AngelList (https://angel.co), Pipeline Angels (https://pipelineangels.com), and Tech Coast Angels (https://www.techcoastangels.com).

18 This website has great information to help you better understand patents and marks: https://www.uspto.gov/.

19 Jeffrey Johnson, "What was the Napster case about and what does the Outcome mean?" FreeAdvice, July 14, 2021, https://www.freeadvice.com/legal/what-was-the-napster-case-about-and-what-does-the-outcome-mean/.

20 Editors of Encyclopaedia Britannica, "IBM," Britannica, https://www.britannica.com/topic/International-Business-Machines-Corporation.

21 "What does ESPN stand for?" ESPN, https://support.espn.com/hc/en-us/articles/360039139792-What-does-ESPN-stand-for-.

22 Denis Collins, "Arthur Andersen," Britannica, February 23, 2023, https://www.britannica.com/topic/Arthur-Andersen.

23 "Employer ID Numbers," September 1, 2022, https://www.irs.gov/businesses/small-businesses-self-employed/employer-id-numbers.

24 "Color Wheel," Canva, https://www.canva.com/colors/color-wheel.

25 Alex Clem, "Raster vs. Vector: What's the Difference and When to Use Which," Shutterstock, November 15, 2021, https://www.shutterstock.com/blog/raster-vs-vector-file-formats.

26 Jerome Conlon, "The Brand Brief Behind Nike's Just Do It Campaign," Branding Strategy Insider, https://brandingstrategyinsider.com/behind-nikes-campaign/#.VdJBCFNVhHz.

27 Ben McClure, "How Venture Capitalists Make Investment Choices," Investopedia, July 26, 2022, https://www.investopedia.com/articles/financial-theory/11/how-venture-capitalists-make-investment-choices.asp.

28 "The Top 12 Reasons Startups Fail," CB Insights, August 3, 2021, https://www.cbinsights.com/research/startup-failure-reasons-top/.

29 Process PA Team, "The Many Different Types of Board of Directors," Process PA, December 17, 2019, https://medium.com/process-pa/the-many-different-types-of-board-of-directors-fdf6f5643dae.

About the Author

Michelle Mink has always had a curious nature and enjoys pushing the envelope. After earning her master's degree from the University of Colorado, Boulder she spent the early part of her career pursuing opportunities during an explosive, transformative time in the telecommunications industry. The period saw a further unraveling of the Ma Bell monopoly, the dot-com boom and the subsequent bust. This gave Michelle opportunities to learn how Fortune 500 companies operate and experience the trial-by-fire world of startups, including taking a company public (via IPO).

After more than two decades of joining, founding and consulting with entrepreneurial ventures, Michelle pinpointed basic startup practices that have caused significant problems for young businesses. Her passion for helping entrepreneurs succeed inspired Michelle to write "Beyond Startup Week: What First-Time Entrepreneurs Don't Know to Ask." She continues to support entrepreneurs on their journeys through Navabiz Solutions. Learn more at **www.navabiz.com**.